JIM LEE

The Ladies of DUNSTER CASTLE

GRAND DAMES, WICKED WIVES AND OTHER TALES OF A HISTORIC CASTLE'S WOMEN

JIM LEE

The Ladies of DUNSTER CASTLE

GRAND DAMES, WICKED WIVES AND OTHER TALES OF A HISTORIC CASTLE'S WOMEN

MEREO
Cirencester

Mereo Books

1A The Wool Market Dyer Street Cirencester Gloucestershire GL7 2PR
An imprint of Memoirs Publishing www.mereobooks.com

The Ladies of Dunster Castle: 978-1-86151-694-7

First published in Great Britain in 2016
by Mereo Books, an imprint of Memoirs Publishing

The address for Memoirs Publishing Group Limited can be found at
www.memoirspublishing.com

The Memoirs Publishing Group Ltd Reg. No. 7834348

The Memoirs Publishing Group supports both The Forest Stewardship Council®
(FSC®) and the PEFC® leading international forest-certification organisations. Our
books carrying both the FSC label and the PEFC® and are printed on FSC®-certified
paper. FSC® is the only forest-certification scheme supported by the leading
environmental organisations including Greenpeace. Our paper procurement policy
can be found at www.memoirspublishing.com/environment

Typeset in 11/16pt Plantin
by Wiltshire Associates Publisher Services Ltd. Printed and bound in Great Britain
by Printondemand-Worldwide, Peterborough PE2 6XD

CONTENTS

Acknowledgements and thanks
Preface
Introduction

PART 1: THE GREAT LADIES OF DUNSTER

PART 2: WOMEN IN TROUBLE

ACKNOWLEDGEMENTS
AND THANKS

Frethesanda: From John Burke's *A Genealogical and Heraldic History of the Commoners of Great Britain and Ireland*, Vol. 1. Henry Colburn, Page 142.

Motherhood, Religion, *Society in Medieval Europe*, 400-1400 (Joan de Mohun Chronicle)

Jocelyn Wogan-Browne Source: *The Cantuarian* (King's School Magazine). Vol 15, No 11, July 1936

Sir Walter Luttrell and Lady Hermione Interview, Editor, *Somerset Life* 1980.

National Trust Sound Archives, Wessex Region, Court House, 1996, Interview by John Fleming.

Kentish Gazette Sep.15th 1923: 'Archaeologists visit "Meister Omers"'

Archaeologia Cantiana Vol. XLVII (1936) – Report of the Canterbury Archaeological Society

History of England (Early Medieval England) – M.T. Clancy 1983

Robin Andrews, Dunster Castle Head Gardener, for further texts on Alys Luttrell and images supplied by Julian Luttrell

Liz Summers, Dunster Castle, Learning Officer, *Illustrious Ladies* draft copies

Hugh Maxwell Lyte: *A History of Dunster Castle / A History of Dunster*, vols 1&2

Dunster Castle – An Illustrated Survey, Text by Mr E. I. Musgrave, revised by Sir Walter Luttrell, English Life Productions 1974

Dudley Dodd, National Trust *An Illustrated Souvenir* 1985

Dudley Dodd, National Trust *Guidebook* 1999

Oliver Garnett, National Trust *Guidebook* 2003

Sarah Douglas, National Trust *Guidebook* 2013

Mohun Chronicle, 14th century – Cistercian Abbot of Newenham in Devon, Walter de la Hove for Joan de Mohun

James Savage: Hundred of Carhampton

The History of Dunster Church and Priory vol 1– Joan Jordan

Oxford Illustrated History of Britain, Edited by Kenneth O. Morgan

Domesday Book – Lady Antonia Fraser

Kings and Queens of England and Scotland - Plantagenet Somerset Fry

The Book of Dunster - Hilary Binding

The Book of Minehead with Alcombe – Hilary Binding

Somerset Place Names – Stephen Robinson

West Somerset Heritage Centre, Taunton

Warwick, The King Maker – A Ladybird Book

Elizabeth the Queen – Alison Weir

Mary Pooley, Sacred Heart Church, Minehead, for translation - History of Parliament

Copley, Thomas (1532-84) of Gatton Surr. - Maxwell Lyte:
History of Dunster - A Changing Community, Hilary Binding

The Luttrells – Glenn Luttrell USA

Further Reading

History of Parliament, Copley, Thomas (1532 -84)

Letters of Sir Thomas Copley

Copley's Gatton 1486-1626

Mary, Queen of Scots, Antonia Fraser 1969

The Oxford History of Britain, Kenneth Morgan 1984

Elizabeth the Queen, Alison Weir 1998

British History, Children's Encyclopedia

The Great Household in Medieval England, C.M. Woolgar

PREFACE

The site of Dunster Castle has been occupied for over one thousand years. The Domesday book of 1086 states that it belonged to Aelfric, a Saxon nobleman at the time of Edward the Confessor. After the Norman Conquest of England, it was granted to William de Mohun, a Norman knight who was companion-in-arms to William the Conqueror. Little survives from the Conquest. The oldest surviving features are the thirteenth century Gateway and semi-circular ruined Bastion tower on Green Court, with twelfth century foundations on some parts of the Keep.

It is generally recognised that Dunster Castle, once a medieval stronghold and now a comfortable country home with dramatic vistas and subtropical gardens, is one of the jewels in the crown of Somerset. Visually impressive, it stands amid the sweeping high hills of Exmoor. Rising from its curtain of woods above the river Avill, it presents a silhouette of formidable towers, battlements and gables against the northern sky, an outline which cannot be excelled for grace. It is equally impressive when seen not from the river and meadow below but from the high street of the quaint little town which struggles up the slope towards its lowest entry. It makes a perfect foreground from which stand out the wooded ascent to its gatehouse and the cluster of towers far above the treetops, yet it evokes the age of siege warfare, cannon fire, dark deeds, bloodshed and treachery.

If the castle's mighty walls could talk they would be telling stories, not of the architects who demolished, rebuilt and added to it, nor of the golden age of chivalry when the castle's knights fought in battle and died, but of romantic rescues, and the scandalous stories and intrigue of the powerful women who propelled the castle through one thousand years of English history and who only recently, through death, finally relinquished their powers. When personal, economic and political obstacles threatened, these women and others like them did not just prevail, they excelled. Their stories are full of adventure, romance, loss, and triumph. They wielded great and lasting influence, and some of them survived decades of social, political and personal upheaval.

Hawis le Fleming, a sister of Humphrey de Bohun, was the first of the Dunster Castle ladies to make an impact by strengthening the medieval defences; one of the curtain wall towers was called Le Fleming Tower in the mid-twelfth century.

In 1376 Lady Joan de Mohun sold Dunster Castle and manors to Lady Elizabeth Luttrell, whose descendant, Elizabeth Courtenay's husband, was charged with high treason, as was she herself during the Wars of the Roses in the latter part of the fifteenth century. Troubles continued with Sir John Luttrell and his wife Mary Rice when he accused her of adultery in 1550. Jane Luttrell blew up Royalist attackers when they tried to storm the castle in 1642 and Mary Luttrell (Tregonwell) had her house in London burnt down in 1696; she was rescued from the inferno by a man who was staying with her, whom she later married.

Dorothy Luttrell made changes to the garden design in the early 1700s, when she built the New Way opposite the stables and commissioned an extravagant classical Georgian chapel to be built on the south terrace. This chapel was demolished to make way for the architect Anthony Salvin during the Victorian rebuilding of many parts of the stronghold and Amelia Ann Hood, mother of Elizabeth Periam Luttrell, granted the village's St Georges' Church £5,000 for its own Victorian restoration.

Alys Luttrell, who came to Dunster Castle in 1920, made many changes to the grounds, both riverside and Keep gardens, and built for herself a beautiful plantation called the Dream Garden, introducing exotic tropical plants most of which survive today and opened gardens to the public to raise money for the Red Cross. Alys died in 1974 and her son Sir Walter Luttrell generously donated the castle and twenty-eight acres of Parkland to the National Trust.

INTRODUCTION

A secluded outpost far from the centre of English politics in London yet frequently to play a key role in the country's affairs, Dunster Castle is unique, spanning almost one thousand years of England's history. Having spoken about the women who helped to shape that history during illustrated slide shows to staff and volunteers whilst I was still working at the castle, I found the prospect of writing about them daunting, but quite irresistible. I am in no doubt as to who the real personages and luminaries were who dominated those centuries, and I hope to say a little more about them than can be found in our guidebooks.

This is my second book on the medieval stronghold at Dunster, following Dunster - A Castle at War (Mereo, 2015), in which the male, either knight or soldier, Parliamentarian or Royalist, was often portrayed as the natural hero, or villain, with the ladies in minor support roles. I now wish to redress that imbalance and give the women the prominent role they richly deserve in an informative and hopefully entertaining way.

The traditional medieval castle has long inspired the imagination, conjuring up images of jousts, banquets, maidens in distress, knights and the golden age of chivalry. Even standing amidst thousand-year-old ruins, it is easy to conjure up the sounds and smells of battles long gone, to imagine the clatter of hooves on the cobbles and to smell the fear rising from the dungeon pits. However, as Dunster's history, in my view, has been so dominated by women, I have taken as my subject those ladies whose inspiration and achievements shaped destiny over the millennia of the castle's history. They are the women of the de Mohun and Luttrell families.

Many of the castle's illustrious ladies had very large families indeed, some of them bearing eight or nine children and three as many as ten. During the Victorian period, in particular, Luttrell families were usually large; after all, Queen Victoria had nine children.

So this book is designed to fill the need for a comprehensive in-print account of the most influential of the Dunster women. Apart from two instances when the castle was lost briefly through the actions of the men, it is thanks to these powerful, determined and brave ladies that the castle remained with the Luttrell family. Their wealth and influence was paramount in shaping the destinies of both castle and village.

The eleven influential women of Dunster who are described in this book did not just prevail when personal, economic and political obstacles threatened –they excelled. Their stories are full of adventure, romance, losses and gains, trials and triumphs.

Not all of these iconic ladies actually resided at Dunster Castle, though most did. At the end of the book I have looked at the lives of a number of less famous women who were associated with Dunster, examining their foibles and temperaments during their occupation and control of the castle and of seduction and corruption. One of the women, a thief and pickpocket, deserves mention for changing the course of Royal protocol. Another helped her husband to fall to his death through a top-floor window. A fourth was almost burnt in a fire, after which she married the sailor who saved her. There are tales of greed, missing gold and silver, of adulteresses, illegal marriages, excommunication, a stillborn child and graveyard gold, a mad housemaid with a knife and a lady walking barefoot over the Exmoor hills at midnight.

This book is not intended to make political comment or rewrite social history on the ladies who graced Dunster Castle from the medieval world to the modern. Instead I have tried to weave enough about them to illustrate and make sense of their stories into existing historical narratives. The reader will find no gossip, but hopefully a sense of purpose and determination shared by the shrewd, intelligent women who steered the castle through tumultuous times to the present day.

A further inspiration was my desire to complement the work of Octavia Hill, an English social reformer whose main concern was the welfare of the inhabitants of cities, especially London, in the second half of the nineteenth century. She also campaigned for the preservation of open spaces, and out of her passionate belief that as a species we need space to breathe arose the National Trust. One of the things I believe women tend to excel at is thinking in the long term, and Octavia had a vision. She was also ahead of her time in her 'eco' thinking. If it wasn't for Octavia Hill, it's unlikely that so many people today would be able to visit historic, beautifully preserved stately homes and similar such properties for a token fee, making history accessible to all.

When I needed an historic iconic female figure in Britain to rally around and help me introduce the illustrious ladies of Dunster Castle I found myself, not surprisingly, surrounded by legions. However, two names stood out head and shoulders above the rest. The first was a striking woman who was tall enough to look any male warrior in the eye, with russet hair tumbling to her waist and a voice that rang out like a bugle call. She was married to the king of the Iceni, a Celtic tribe and she was of royal blood, a queen in her own right. Her name means 'Victorious' and she was revered as both a leader and a priestess. She was of course Boudicca, the first British woman we know of with real attitude. The Romans created this mythic, flame-haired über-woman in an attempt to explain how a woman could have come so close to defeating them. She must have looked a breathtaking sight when she rode into battle on her chariot. A genuine British heroine, she embodied a very British sense of freedom.

Boudicca was "huge of frame, terrifying of aspect, and with a harsh voice. A great mass of bright red hair fell to her knees: She wore a great twisted golden necklace, and a tunic of many colours, over which was a thick mantle, fastened by a brooch. Now she grasped a spear, to strike fear into all who watched her..." (Cassius Dio, Roman historian).

Boudicca on her chariot with her two daughters – bronze sculpture, Westminster, London

The second is Britannia. In that stirring, quintessentially British image — trident raised, hair cascading from beneath a plumed Corinthian helmet, breasts proudly bared (at least until the prudent Victorians covered them up) — is the personification of our national character. From mystical beginnings more than 2,000 years ago, Britannia has become, as the historian Roy Matthews writes, "part of the collective consciousness of the island kingdom... with a place deep in the hearts and minds of the people".

Cleopatra, the last Egyptian Pharaoh, exerted her own unique power. She was a member of the Ptolemaic dynasty, a family of Macedonian Greek origin that ruled Egypt after Alexander the Great's death during the Hellenistic period. Her tragic story is theatrically shown in glorious colour in the Leather Gallery at Dunster Castle. Mark Antony, one of the three rulers of the Roman Empire, spent his time in Egypt, living a life of decadence and conducting an affair with the country's beautiful queen, who (according to tradition) killed herself by inducing a snake to bite her.

These were all strong, spirited women whose transcendental lives and legendary stories have elevated mankind with their mystique, their beauty, their wisdom, wit, virtue, grace, talent, kindness or exceptional courage. They were legendary and semi-legendary goddesses. None of our ladies, as far as I'm aware, were sword-wielding heroines, though one did fire cannons in earnest.

My main qualification for writing this book is that I have been immersed in these women's stories for so many years. I have tried to be as accurate as possible, given the demands of brevity. Dunster Castle's history is a vast canvas, and there are so many aspects to it that my hardest task is choosing what to include and what to leave out. The details I have included are therefore those that best portray the ladies mentioned and which best illustrate their many and varied characters. Whilst the men may have shone on faraway battlefields, the women stole the spotlight at home by making the equivalent of banner headlines.

This book is dedicated to all volunteers, new
and nearly new, past and future at Dunster Castle.

PART 1
The great ladies of Dunster

CHAPTER 1

FRETHESANDA (FRETHESANT) PAGANEL

1160-1232

'A willowy, queenly lady'

Frethesanda lived in an age just after the Norman Conquest, when the Anglo-Norman elite were the heirs of William and his conquerors and formed a tightly-knit community. They succeeded in holding on to power by adopting and adapting to new circumstances whilst drawing at the same time on the French culture to which they owed their roots. French remained the principle language of the aristocracy, whilst Latin was the language of education. So confident and successful was this Anglo-Norman elite that they spread west and north into Wales, Scotland and Ireland.

Frethesanda belonged to a well-known Norman family who established themselves from Anglia to West Somerset and the Quantock Hills and met up with Luttrells along the way.

To know a little about how the area of Court House descended upon the latter it is necessary to say a little of the main homesteads, including East Quantoxhead. There are three main farms in the parish of East Quantoxhead. Townsend Farm lies just off the very busy A39, whereas Court Farm can be found on the quiet approach to the village. Perry Farm is a couple of kilometres away and lies on the edge of the sister parish of West Quantoxhead (or St Audries). The farms are all still working farms. Up until the beginning of the 20th century the village was a thriving community, self-supporting with shops, school and an inn (it was called the New Inn, but became redundant in 1916 and is now known as Prospect House). Since 1861 the population of the village has declined from 339 to about 100.

The village, being part of Court House Estate, has not changed very much. This is partly because it has been in private ownership, so there has been no enforced new development. In the 1920s special legislation had to be used to allow the local council to build its quota of two houses on land it did not own.

The Village Hall was opened in 1914 in memory of Alice Luttrell, who was the wife of the then squire, Alexander Luttrell. Before this there had been a small dame school (Quantocks Education, 'The Changing Village') on the site. The church of St Mary's lies next to the Manor House, the most impressive building in the village.

Court House has descended in an unbroken family line through the Luttrells from 1086 to the present day, first becoming their property when Andrew Luttrell inherited from Frethesanda in 1232. It then became the secondary home of the family until Elizabeth Luttrell acquired Dunster Castle in 1376. The manor house was let from 1666 until 1888, when they returned.

Frethesanda Paganel's name comes first in all pedigree charts of the Luttrell family at Dunster Castle. Look in any of the genealogy lists contained in guide books and there she is, proudly married to Geoffrey Luttrell (d.1216) first and foremost. Her name comes from the French for the Anglo Saxon name Fridyswyde. The two families had known each other since the Norman Conquest and possibly in France too. The Luttrells descended from a Norman baron who accompanied Duke William in his conquest of England.

The Paganel family come from the great barons of Normandy and crossed to Hastings with William the Conqueror in 1066. They soon established themselves. Frethesanda, a unique name, is the French form of the Anglo Saxon Frediswyde or Frideswyde, meaning 'peace' or 'strong '. St Frideswide was an 8th century English princess who is credited with establishing Christ Church in Oxford.

Frethesanda Luttrell (born Paganel or Paynel) was born in 1160 in Hooton Pagnel, West Riding, Yorkshire, to

William Paynel (Paganel) and Frethesanda de Mucheney. She is the first of the illustrious ladies to be mentioned because the Luttrells' subsequent fortune was founded on this beautiful young heiress of 17 years of age from Yorkshire whom Sir Geoffrey Luttrell of Gamston, south Nottinghamshire, married in 1187. During the absence of King Richard the Lionheart, who was on Crusade in the Holy Land fighting Saladin the Muslim leader, Geoffrey Luttrell went into open rebellion with Richard's younger brother, Prince John, later King. On Richard I's return from Palestine, Luttrell was deprived of all his lands, though he had them all reinstated after the accession of Prince John to the Crown in 1199.

This was also the time when the Robin Hood legend was created and when the Luttrell family enter into recorded English history alongside the Sheriff of Nottingham, Sherwood Forest and 'bad' King John. In the latter part of the twelfth century Geoffrey Luttrell had acquired properties at Gamston and Bridgeford in Nottingham, close to Sherwood Forest and Clumber Park, now in the care of the National Trust.

Not too much is known about Frethesanda herself. Her family had lands in the East Riding, West Riding and North Riding as well as in Lincolnshire and Leicestershire, as borne out by the Domesday Survey of 1086. At this time the Luttrells had small properties in Gamston and Bridgeford, near to each other and to the River Trent in Nottinghamshire. Bridgeford was chosen as the administrative centre for Nottinghamshire County Council.

The 13th century saw great progress in the dyeing and working of wool, which was by far the most important material for outerwear. For the rich, colour was very important. Blue was introduced and became very fashionable, being adopted by the Kings of France as their heraldic colour. Dress for Frethesanda was modest and restrained. A floor-length, loosely-fitted gown, with long, tight sleeves and a narrow belt was uniform. Over it was worn the 'cyclas', or sleeveless surcoat. Wealthy women wore more embroidery and their mantle, held in place by a cord across the chest, might be lined with fur. Women, like men, wore hose and leather shoes.

It is noted in some descendancy charts that Frethesanda was born in Nottingham Castle and died at Irnham Castle. Irnham has no castle, though it does have the impressive Irnham Hall, owned by the Paganels since the Norman Conquest, which subsequently passed to the Luttrells in the early 13th century. The original Manor House was built by the Luttrell family, who owned the estate prior to 1419. Irnham was one of the fifteen manors given by William the Conqueror to Ralph Paganel, and it passed from his family via the heiress, Frethesant Paynel (the French spelling) to her son, Sir Andrew Luttrell, Knight. 1st Baron of Irnham. There is a road in Minehead called Irnham Road.

Frethesanda was daughter and coheiress of William Paganel, and although he was only a younger scion of the great family of Paynell, she and her sister Isabel Bastard inherited from him fifteen knights' fees, mainly in

Yorkshire. Her total inheritance included property in the counties of York, Derby, Nottingham, Lincoln and East Quantoxhead in Somerset, all of which passed to the Luttrell family. This estate, nine miles to the east of Dunster Castle, affords yet another startling instance of land tenure in England with the Victorian George Luttrell, through only two females, the lineal descendant of Sir Ralph Paynel, who had held Court House, East Quantoxhead, since William the Conqueror.

The dress worn by Frethesanda

Her small hamlet of East Quantoxhead seems caught in a time capsule. It lies just off the main A39 and on the edge of the Bristol Channel. The village centre has a feeling of great tranquillity with its exquisite manor house and church, thatched cottages, medieval barns and its own duck pond and old mill building.

The village has a long history. In Saxon times it was included in the "Royal Hundreds" of Williton and was well defended by King Alfred from the Danes who would attack the coastal villages. After the Norman

Conquest it was given to the Paganel family and later passed to the Luttrell family in 1189 when Geoffrey Luttrell married the Paganel heiress. It's tempting to think Frethesanda actually walked in the same courtyard next to the Manor House. The parish of East Quantoxhead was part of the Williton and Freemanners Hundred.

The village has a manor house, church, thatched cottages, medieval tithe barn, its own duck pond and mill house dating from 1725. The manor house, known as Court House, has a medieval tower and other parts of the building date from the 17th century. It has been designated as a Grade I listed building. The manor was granted to Ralph Pagnall after the Norman Conquest passing down through generations to the Luttrells. No part of the estate has been sold since its grant around 1070 and is still owned by the descendants of the Paganel and Luttrell families. This required a special Act of Parliament in the 1920s to enable council houses to be built on land which was not freehold, contrary to the rules in the rest of the country.

The village used to have a small harbour which brought in limestone for local limekilns and exported alabaster. It is thought that it was also used for smuggling.

At some time before 1725 Perry Hill was the site of a copper mine.

The Court House building is listed under the Planning (Listed Buildings and Conservation Areas) Act 1990 as amended for its special architectural or historic interest.

Other accounts of Frethesanda include the report that on 26 February, 1203:

A fine was levied between Geoffrey Luttrell and Frethesant his wife and Isabel, Frethesant's sister, plaintiffs, and Agnes de Triberge (Thrybergh), tenant, of 4 bovates and 30 acres of land in Hooton Pagnell. Agnes recognized the land to be the right of Frethesant and Isabel, by the service of a fortieth part of a knight's fee. On 27 February of the same year a fine was levied between the same plaintiffs and Ellis, abbot of Kirkstall, tenant, of 11 bovates and 80 acres of land in the same place, being all the land which the abbot had held of the fee of William Paynel there the abbot recognized the land to be the right of Frethesant and Isabel, and quitclaimed it to the plaintiffs, who in return granted to him and the convent all the land which the abbot and convent had in the soke of Adel of the gift of William Mustel and his ancestors, being of the fee of Frethesant and Isabel, and all the tenements they could acquire in future of the said fee the plaintiffs gave the abbot 30 marks of silver. On the same day, the same plaintiffs grant to Osmund, abbot of Roche, and the convent 12 bovates of land in Thurnscoe the abbot giving 8 marks of silver.

Sir Geoffrey Luttrell died in 1216 or 1217. On 15 May, 1218 the Sheriff of Yorkshire was ordered to take security from Henry de Newmarch for 40 marks which he had undertaken to pay for having as his wife Frethesant, widow of Geoffrey Luttrell, should she be willing, and to give him 'seisin' (possession of freehold land) of her lands. This denotes the legal possession of a feudal fiefdom or fee, that is to say an estate in land.

Frethesant Paynel occurs as the wife of Henry de Newmarch in 1219 when her lands included a moiety (half share) of Barton (-le-Street) in Ryedale wapentake, a moiety of (Nether) Silton in Birdforth wapentake, and 10 pounds' worth of land in Stratforth wapentake. On 29 October, 1219 the Sheriff of Yorkshire was ordered to give seisin to Frethesant daughter and heir of William Paynel of the lands of her father in Hooton Pagnell and Shilton (presumably Nether Shilton) which fell to her by hereditary right.

Henry de Newmarch was dead in 1239, and Frethesant

appear to have married Roger de Triberge or Thrybergh. In 1240 Roger de Triberge and Frethesant his wife quitclaimed for themselves and their heirs to Andrew Luttrell and his heirs a moiety of the manor of Hooton Pagnell and all the lands and tenements which were of the heritage of William Paynel, and Andrew granted them land in Hooton, to hold to them and the heirs of Frethesant of him and his heirs.

In defining the private sphere, the scope of a woman's self-interest included wives and mothers working to advance the interests of their spouses and children. Simply by Frethesant's management of the household she allowed her spouse to leave home and give his service for the crown, which in turn could supply him with prestige and power through his military endeavours. A medieval woman could be forced to use many methods, not always acceptable ones, to reach a desired outcome. The contribution of money and support through dowry, wage labour, household works, production, patronage and hospitality were many of the acceptable ways.

The use of affection within her household gave her influence because it could directly result in loyalty to her. Wifely persuasion could be used, for example to persuade a spouse to donate funds to the church. Her offspring could also be influenced through her motherly guidance. Her use of sexual attraction to influence not only her husband but also other members of the opposite sex may have worked to her benefit. There were other unattractive means for her to gain influence that were feared and unaccepted, but which had to be used occasionally. Gossip could often result in a desired end, along with plain old lying or deceit.

Frethesanda's ancestral name Paganel is emblazoned in Minehead on street names such as Paganel Road, Paganel View and Close and Paganel Way. Dying in 1240, she outlived her husband by some 24 years. Their name still survives in Hooton Pagnell, Boothby Pagnell and Newport Pagnell.

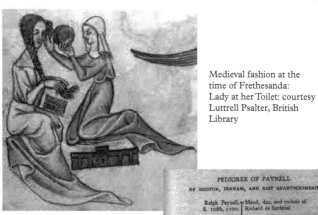

Medieval fashion at the time of Frethesanda: Lady at her Toilet: courtesy Luttrell Psalter, British Library

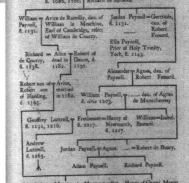

The Paynell pedigree - Hugh Maxwell Lyte

CHAPTER 2

JOAN DE MOHUN AND HER 14TH CENTURY CHRONICLE

Joan de Mohun, 1330-1404

Although historical sources about medieval women are not as numerous as those relating to men, they are much richer than is often supposed. Surviving documents, literary and other texts and images make it clear that medieval women were resilient, resourceful and skilled. Moreover, in exceptional instances they were capable of exercising political power, learning and creativity outside the domestic sphere.

In illustration of the remarkable position occupied by Lady de Mohun during her husband's lifetime, we might notice a royal grant to her of a wardship while she was 'feme convert', which meant that, upon marriage, a woman's legal rights and obligations were subsumed by those of her husband, in accordance with the wife's legal status.

Joan de Mohun's story is set against the military and political turmoil of the age. The Hundred Years War with France was engulfing England's economy during this series of wars interspersed with truces. It was during one such truce, in 1375, that Joan's husband, Sir John de Mohun V, died leaving no male heir. The following year Joan sold off the reversion of Dunster Castle and moved to the Court of Richard II and the hallowed halls of Canterbury Cathedral. This was also the century of the bubonic plague known as the Black Death, which devastated England, causing horrific suffering.

Joan is arguably the best known of all the medieval ladies at Dunster Castle and has been a personal favourite of mine since we first 'met'. Her story captures the imagination in legend and in fact. She was a lady of great renown, and a great favourite at court who had six maidservants of her own.

In his book The Court of Richard II, Father Gervase Mathew stated that Joan, Lady Mohun, was one of the most influential ladies of Richard's court. King Richard's queen, Anne of Bohemia and Hungary, was a personal friend, and one of her last acts was to grant Lady Mohun Leeds Castle, in Kent. Queen Anne spent that Christmas with Joan in Leeds Castle. Joan knew she had influence, direct and indirect, and knew how to use it. According to John Osborne, Joan's clerk, Constable of Dunster Castle and author of a Mohun registrar, the Abbot of Newenham had given accounts of the Mohun events in his Red Book for the utility and profits of the Lords of Dunster and most of all to the praise and glory of his most noble Lady, Joan de Mohun. This book is probably identifiable with the Mohun Chronicle.

There was a life cycle to a woman's authority. As a maid, Joan's power grew with the inheritance of land. As a wife, this power waned with marriage, when her lands and legal status went to her husband. As a widow, it increased again when she became the head of the household. Widows, owed suit to court, answered complaints and pursued litigation without the intervention of a man. Widows were sought after for marriage. If a man could persuade a widow to marry him it could mean an increase in wealth and power among influential families for himself and his family. Once widowed, a woman was responsible for her own lands until she remarried. Many chose to remain widows, a reasonable choice under the circumstances. Widowed women had legal independence and, in many instances, autonomy over considerable financial resources. Not only were estates held for years by widows but in some cases waste and loss of land also occurred.

Many widows proved to be good administrators, but not all. The inheritance of Thomas de Courtenay, Earl of Devon, was seriously wasted during his minority by the administration headed by his mother and even when he came of age his mother retained two thirds of his estates as her jointure and dower until her death in 1441.

It was rare and very difficult for a widow to get rid of the whole family inheritance. It was always accepted that dower was held by the widow for her lifetime, and King Edward I's legislation provided for the heir to recover alienated dower. The succession to jointure lands was laid down in the marriage settlement or other deeds, and according to feudal custom the woman's inheritance passed to the heir by right of primogeniture. Lady Joan de Mohun was exceptional in disposing of the family lands by sale, making use of the device of enfeoffment in order to do so.

In 1369 Joan's husband Sir John de Mohun, conveyed his principle estates to feoffees on the condition that they followed his wife's orders in disposing of them. Sir John died six years later, leaving three daughters who had already made good marriages but no son. Before his death Joan had agreed to sell the lands to Elizabeth Luttrell, and she carried this out in 1376; the feoffees conveyed the lands to her for life with remainder to Lady Elizabeth Luttrell. Therefore Joan continued the income from her estates and also had the original purchase money of £3,333. 6s 8d; her daughters and their husbands had, however, no inheritance to look forward to.

Debt might also be a serious problem, and it was for this reason that Joan de Mohun sold Dunster Castle to Elizabeth Luttrell one year after the death of Sir John de Mohun, whose attitude to family and social affairs left a lot to be desired. Incompatibility is difficult to gauge from the evidence, but many husbands and wives had to come to terms with unfaithfulness, and there was little Joan could have done if her husband took another partner.

There were many aspects to a medieval woman's life which I will not discuss here, all of them centring on her ability to see the chance for use of power and utilize it to her fullest capabilities. We may not necessarily like some of the routes she took, but they were very necessary at the time in order for a woman to at least have her own personal opinions and designs come into reality. She was restricted, but not as oppressed as movies and many romantic fiction novels would have us believe medieval women were. They were very similar to the women of today, looking out for the interests of the family and working to have a voice in society.

Joan de Mohun's Chronicle is an incomplete Anglo Norman prose composed by the Cistercian Abbot of Newenham, Devon, founded by Reynold de Mohun 11 in 1245, and written for Joan de Mohun. This mid-fourteenth century chronicle acknowledges female roles in the memory and history of a family. One medieval manuscript from the Chronicle survives (BL, add. 62929). The Chronicle illustrates Lady Joan's legendary strength of character, fortitude and status. She was the daughter of Bartholomew Burghersh the elder, who was a soldier, diplomatic envoy and chamberlain to King Edward III. It was her uncle, Henry Burghersh, Bishop of Lincoln and Chancellor of England, who obtained the marriage of John de Mohun V and custody of his land. They married on or just before 1341. In that year John de Mohun was given livery of his inheritance, the lordship of Dunster Castle.

Sir John did extremely well as a military man fighting against both the Scots and the French in 1346 and 1347. He was very much part of Edward the Black Prince's household, of which his father was the master, and part of the close-knit group of earls, barons and knights who fought at the Battle of Crecy in 1346, all original members of the 25 knights in the renowned Order of the Garter. Yet Sir John, although regularly summoned to Parliament, and once to a council, held only commissions in his own Somerset region and no civilian office at Court: he does not seem to have been as successful in peacetime as in war. He was often in trouble with others in his own estates and was indicted for various felonies and got into serious trouble for by attempting to interfere with the due process of law. One of his military tenants of the Honour of Dunster brought a suit against him to recover some lands, and when the King's judges were sitting at Somerton to hear this and other cases, Sir John attacked his adversary in the middle of the town, pursued him as far as the churchyard and, overtaking him carried him off on horseback to Langport. Such violence could not be tolerated even in a great baron, and, by order of the judge the sheriff raised a hue and cry against him and rescued his captive. Sir John was committed to prison, receiving a royal pardon at a later date. As a baron he failed his family in custodianship and succession, spending his inheritance as soon as he got it. He died with debts outstanding and produced no male heir.

The Mohun Chronicle may well be seen in the context

of the very real threats of instability both felt and resisted by the Mohuns, dependent as they were on traditional landholding, but not evidently producing enough income to carry on much longer. They were soon manoeuvring to hold onto Sir John's inheritance, largely by transferring it temporarily to his wife, Joan. From 1346 to 1350 they conveyed, reconveyed and mortgaged Dunster Castle and soon the Mohun lands fell into her hands; by 1355 Sir John had made over to his wife forty-three title deeds relating to their Dunster manors and other holdings.

A 14th century 'noble lady' costume such as that which would have been worn by Joan de Mohun

However, although Dunster Castle had been mortgaged, the astute marriage between Joan's eldest daughter, the six-year-old Elizabeth de Mohun and the Earl of Salisbury had been made in 1349 and Sir John's successful relations with his fellow soldiers and relatives in the royal circle were being consolidated both by this marriage and his inclusion in the founding members of the Order of the Garter affirmed the Mohun's ancient right to belong at the heart of the elite. Her vision of the past is for female foundresses for a family where daughters were the future so here were reasons for turning to the past to affirm present prestige and to try to build a future.

As we have noted her husband, John de Mohun, had died in 1375. One year later, Joan completed the sale of her own life-interest in Dunster Castle to Elizabeth Luttrell for a large sum and shut up the castle on its Somerset Tor.

Original sale of receipt of Dunster Castle 1376 to be seen in Morning Room. Translation:

Let all people who see or hear this writing know that I, Joan, widow of John de Mohun of Dunster, have received from Elizabeth, widow of Sir Andrew Luttrell, five thousand marks of good money in full payment for the castle of Dunster and the manors of Minehead, Kilton and Carhampton with the hundred of Carhampton and all their appurtenances. Of which five thousand marks I acknowledge that I have been well and properly satisfied and that the said Elizabeth is quit hereby. In witness of which fact I have set my seal to this document.

Dated at London on the twentieth day of November in the fiftieth year of the reign of King Edward III

She went off to spend what turned out to be a widowhood of some thirty years at court and in Canterbury. With the castle closed, the farms virtually ceased to exist. The demesne was let in sections and the rents were sent to Joan in London or Kent. Under these circumstances it would have been difficult to maintain an effective claim upon the services of the tied servant or villein. By 1377, only one year after Joan left Dunster Castle, the number of autumn works in this manor had fallen. Under this system Joan got 2s 6d from every acre sown in the spring and reaped in the summer, with something additional for the right of turning sheep and cattle on the land in autumn and winter. Each of the great fields was allowed to lie fallow for one year.

Joan outlived Elizabeth Luttrell, who never had her side of the bargain in person, although the Luttrell family did get Dunster Castle eventually. Joan de Mohun was held in high favour by King Richard II, son of the Black Prince, and Queen Ann of Bohemia and continued skilfully dealing in land and money with them both, exchanging an annuity by which her service was rewarded for the manor of Macclesfield and later acquiring the lease of Leeds Castle in Kent.

It is worth noting that at the same time Sir Hugh Luttrell was Constable of Leeds. He was to take on the de Mohun family five years later in a bitter wrangle over the ownership of Dunster Castle after the death of Joan in 1404.

Like some other widows and daughters of the founding

Knights of the Garter, Joan and her daughter, now Countess of Salisbury, were given livery of the Order of the Garter in 1384. Joan was among the three ladies of court compelled to renounce the court by the Appellants in their purge of Richard II's counsellors in 1387.

The presence of women like Joan at Richard's court became more common, and from the beginning of his reign women were regularly elected to the sorority of the Garter. This sisterhood of women espoused certain fraternal principles (or lack thereof). They patterned themselves on male organizations and were known as sister or parallel groups to specific fraternities. They did all the things fraternities do, and by the time of Richard's reign the Court was shedding the character of a militarised household and, again thanks to Joan, was evolving into the sophisticated, civilised court of the Renaissance, paving the way for the Tudors.

On 23 April 2006, St George's Day, the Duke of York and the Earl of Wessex were both made Royal Knights of the Garter by Her Majesty the Queen. Prince Andrew and Prince Edward were both appointed to this the most senior British order of chivalry amid a weekend of celebrations to mark Her Majesty's 80th birthday. This high honour recognised their seniority within the Royal Family and joined their father HRH Prince Philip, their brother HRH The Prince of Wales and sister The Princess Royal in the Order, followed more recently by HRH Prince William of Wales.

Joan died in 1404 but was not buried beside her

husband; she had commissioned her own stone monument in Edward, the Black Prince's Chapel of Our Lady in the crypt of Canterbury Cathedral. This she had inscribed with both her maiden and her married name: 'Johane de Borwasche ke feut dam de Mohun'. The monument shows her not in widow's garb but in fashionable low-cut clothing with jewelled buttons, a woman who had prospered by financial acuity, by trading in, not holding on to land, and by using the skills of a courtier in her successful service as a lady in waiting – a woman, that is, who had organised a different future for herself once her husband, John de Mohun, had gone to the grave and with him, her lineage responsibilities.

In 1395, Lady de Mohun entered into a formal agreement with the Prior and Convent of Christ Church, Canterbury, that her body should be buried in the tomb which she had prepared, and never removed therefrom. One of the monks was to say mass daily for nine specified persons at the altar of St. Mary, or on certain great festivals, at the altar of St. John Baptist near the famous tomb of St. Thomas. For this service he was to receive £2 a year, and the clerk in charge of the chapel was to receive 5s. a year for keeping the tomb clean and in good condition. On the eve of the anniversary of her death, placebo and duruge were to be sung. On the anniversary, a solemn mass of requiems was to be said, the celebrant receiving 6s.8d. and the other two clergy 3s.4d. apiece. A hundred poor people were also to receive 1d. apiece.

In consideration of the benefits promised, Lady de

Mohun gave to the monks 350 marks, a set of three vestments of green "sendal", two choir-copes of cloth of gold valued at £20, a missal worth £5 and a chalice worth £2, besides a bed worth £20 of white and red "camaka", with four cushions of the same, a covering lined with blue silk and curtains of "sedal" of Genoa and Tripoli.

Of the nine persons for whom masses were to be said, four were living in 1395: Richard, King of England, Lady Joan de Mohun, the foundress of the Chantry, 'Elizabeth', presumably the Countess of Salisbury, her daughter, and Elizabeth le Despencer, her niece. The other five persons already deceased were 'John', doubtless her husband, 'Edward', perhaps the late King, another 'Edward', either the Black Prince or the husband of her niece, and Philippa and Anne, Queens of England. The omission from the list of her deceased daughter Maud, her living daughter Philippa and her living grandson Richard le Strange is significant.

When Lady de Mohun felt her end approaching, she sent for the Prior of Christ Church and delivered to him a closed box, to be entrusted to the two monks who acted as guardians of the shine (feretri) of St. Thomas. The box contained the royal letters patent of 1369, and various important documents connected with the sale of Dunster, Minehead, Kilton and Carhampton. Conscious that there was likely to be trouble about her action in this matter, she bound the Prior to deliver the box to her heirs or to Sir Hugh Luttrell if either they or he got possession of the property without opposition, or to the successful party if there should be a suit at law.

On the same day, Lady de Mohun made her will, at a house in the precincts of Canterbury known as Master Omer's. To the Archbishop of Canterbury, whom she nominated an executor, she bequeathed a psalter cover with white, and to her son-in-law the Duke of York a fair copy of the Legenda Sanctorum and another illuminated book. To his wife she left her blessing, suggestive of a previous estrangement, and her best ruby. Her other daughter, the Countess of Salisbury, was to have her favourite cross and a second copy of the Legenda Sanctorum, and Lady le Despencer the elder was to have a bed of green silk. The only other relation mentioned was William Burghersh.

To the Prior of Christ Church she bequeathed some old hangings embroidered with lions and some "ystayned" hangings. One of her mantles was to be reserved for the wife of Sir Thomas Hawkwood. Friar John, her own confessor, was to receive 10 marks, and another Franciscan friar named Henry, 40s. There were further legacies to her six maidservants, to Philip Caxton her clerk, to John Sumpterman and John Gardener and other men who were presumably in her service. Provision was also made for the maintenance of three young scholars then at Canterbury. Every poor person coming to her funeral was to receive 1d. and on that occasion twelve poor men clothed in black at her expense were to hold torches, in addition to the four great candles weighing 20lb. that were to burn during the ceremony. All goods not otherwise disposed of were bequeathed to the church of Canterbury.

Two days after making the will to the foregoing effect, on the 4th of October 1404, Lady de Mohun died. The will was made at a house known as Meister Omers, in the Precincts of Canterbury. We have a painting which her head rests upon two tasselled cushions supported by angels. The crown is encircled with a richly jewelled garland and a jewelled frontlet stretched across her forehead. A great mass of hair enclosed in a fret, or jewelled net, descends on both sides of the face to the level of the chin.

Illustration by
H Maxwell Lyte KCB (painting)

As Lady Joan had long since cast off all signs of widowhood, she does not wear a barbe or pleated face veil her neck is quite bare. A row of ten very large buttons adorn the close-fitting tunic of brocade known as the cote-hardie, without sleeves and cut away for a considerable space beneath the arm-holes, thus revealing part of a jewelled girdle. Beneath is a kirtle reaching down to the feet, and there are remains of an outer mantle hanging from the shoulders. The lion at her feet is unfortunately mutilated, and her hands have been broken off since 1726. The dateless inscription, repeated on either side, shows the pride which, even as an aged

Lady Joan de Mohun rests within the undercroft at Canterbury Cathedral

widow, she took in her maiden name: *Mor dieux priez larne Johane de Burchersh ne faut dame de Mohun.*

Extracts from an essay by Jocelyn Wogan Browne:

Joan's widowhood could be viewed as the celebration of the family, declared, not on male, but on female heirs. However, Joan's aims seemed to have had less to do with this and more to do with financial security and domestic comfort and displaying the pleasures and sociability, power and influence. Joan's own career seems to have fluctuated between centres and powers of influence at the court of King Edward III and Richard II, the outlying provinces of Somerset, then back to London and Canterbury. From a failing barony (of Sir John de Mohun) to an intimate position of favour at Court, where in some ways, still at the margins of political centre, she is also, as her Garter Robes, expulsion and return, suggest a figure of emblematic importance and resonance.

CHAPTER 3

WARS OF THE ROSES: THE TRIALS AND TRIBULATIONS OF ELIZABETH LUTTRELL

Elizabeth Luttrell, ??-1493

The trials, tribulations and sheer endurance of Elizabeth Luttrell without doubt gain her a place in our roll-call of the great women of Dunster.

The name 'Wars of the Roses' is based on the badges used by the quarrelsome and warring factions between the two sides of the same Plantagenet dynasty, the red rose for the Lancastrians and the white rose for York. The Earl of Somerset, House of Lancaster and the Duke of York, House of York, were seen quarrelling bitterly in a garden about their family's fortunes. Somerset gathered a rose and said, "Let those who are friends to the House of

Lancaster wear a red rose," whereupon the Duke of York immediately plucked a rose. "And those of mine, a white!" he cried.

But the Wars of the Roses had their origins in the Hundred Years War with France. The name the 'Hundred Years' War' has been used by historians to describe the long conflict that pitted the kings and kingdoms of France and England against each other from 1337 to 1453. These were the same wars that Joan of Arc, a young peasant girl, was born into before she helped the French at the siege of Orléans. She was eventually captured by the Burgundians, then sold to the English, who tried her for witchcraft and heresy and burned her at the stake. The long war had been waged by the House of Lancaster.

The Luttrell family of Dunster Castle had been staunch supporters of the House of Lancaster ever since Sir Hugh Luttrell, who built the Great Gatehouse, was an esquire in the household of John of Gaunt, son of Edward III. In July 1433 King Edward VI sold to the Earl of Stafford for 400 marks the right of tendering in marriage to James Luttrell, who had been a ward of court, a lady of suitable rank. This lady was to be Elizabeth Courtenay, daughter of Sir Philip Courtenay, who had been James Luttrell's guardian, and they were duly married at Exeter by the Bishop in the private chapel of Powderham Castle on 13th January 1451.

The choice of lady for Sir James Luttrell could not have been more illustrious. Elizabeth came from a long line of nobility connected directly to the Kings and Queens of

England. Her ancestor Hugh Courtenay married Margaret de Bohun, grand-daughter of King Edward I and Queen Eleanor of Castille. The Courtenay family became the most influential in the West Country, at one time having four castles, including Okehampton. Sir Hugh Courtenay had succeeded as 2nd Earl in 1335, an obvious royal affirmation of their pre-eminence in society.

The swan supporters, ducally gorged and chained on Luttrell's Arms of Achievement also derive from the Courtenay family (see the stone heraldic tablet above the entrance porch). The Luttrell family are amongst the few commoners in England to have heraldic supporters, the prerogative of peers and the Crown. The swan, in turn, derives from the medieval world and the Feast of the Swan, a chivalric celebration of the knighting of 267 men at Westminster Abbey on 22 May 1306.

Luttrell Arms of Achievement. Note the swan supporters either side of the Luttrell badge, which derive from Elizabeth Courtenay's family with royalty. They can also be seen above Dunster Castle's entrance Porch. The motto reads 'That which is taken by war must be held by skill'.

It followed a call to arms by Edward I of England to take revenge on the Scots and their leader, Robert the Bruce. The King first knighted his son, Edward II, who in turn knighted the 266 others. At the feast that followed, the King had two golden swans brought in on a silver platter, and the men were knighted during the banquet, the largest mass knighting in medieval England. The event was described by one contemporary chronicler as the most splendid since King Arthur himself was crowned.

In 1447 King Henry VI had promised that James Luttrell would receive possession of Dunster Castle and estates without James having to prove he was of full age. All seemed to be going well for the young knight and his lady after their eventual marriage in 1450 at Powderham Castle. Little did Elizabeth know that her lavish lifestyle, cosseted world and royal ancestry would, within a few years, come crashing down upon her head. The trials and tribulations of Lady Elizabeth Luttrell began soon after the Wars of the Roses broke out in 1455 and continued for almost forty years. From 1463 to 1485 and the fall of the House of York on the battlefield at Bosworth, Elizabeth Luttrell was neither in possession of her castle nor her estates. Even in those distracted times of civil war there could not have been many widows who had lost two husbands, both brutally killed fighting on behalf of the unfortunate House of Lancaster, leading to the loss of her castle and all her possessions at Dunster. Not only that, but her immediately family, the Courtenays, were in deadly peril of losing all in Devon. To rub salt into her wounds, Elizabeth Luttrell was now known only as the 'farmer of the manor of Minehead'.

Elizabeth's first husband, Sir James Luttrell, wearing his red rose proudly, had fought with distinction at the Battle of Wakefield alongside Henry VI. At the second Battle of St Albans in 1460 he was knighted on the field of battle, under the glorious Lancastrian banner of Queen Margaret. When the fighting was fiercest he was cut deeply with a battleaxe to the neck and shoulder and died in agony a few days later from his wounds.

Family grief was eclipsed by news that the Lancastrian king, Henry VI, had been deposed and that Edward of York was now king. The treason of Sir James Luttrell and the tragedy of Lady Elizabeth Luttrell began soon after. Her fate was sealed when the Parliament that sat in November 1461 passed a sweeping ordinance against all the chief supporters of the House of Lancaster. It singled out for severe criticism Sir James Luttrell, along with his companion-in arms, for their part in the Battle of Wakefield, stating that Sir James *'With grete despite and cruell violence, with horrible and unmanly tyrannye murdered the late Duke of York at Wakefield and to stand and be convicted and attainted of high treason, and forfeit to the King and his heires all the castles and manors and other lands of which they were or had been possessed'.*

Sir James was of course already dead, but high treason carried a duel penalty; death and seizure of estates. A horrible custom in those days was to cut off the heads of traitors and mount them on pikes over the village, town or city from whence they came. Queen Margaret had the head of the Duke of York, murdered by Luttrell and his knights, set upon the gates of the city of York. One can only imagine the anguish of Lady Luttrell had Sir James's head been set on a pike in Dunster village.

Dunster Castle during the Wars of the Roses, 1460: Painting by Ivan Lapper

Consequently Dunster Castle was held forfeit and given to the king's favourite, Sir William Herbert, future Earl of Pembroke. Lady Elizabeth was thrown unceremoniously out of the castle, homeless and with a young family to bring up, Alexander, Hugh, Jane and two more unnamed daughters. Although the wardship and marriage of the young Alexander were taken by the Crown, it made no impact on Lady Elizabeth and her remaining children.

The young Wiliam Herbert's lands were entrusted to his mother in recompense for her dower, the property of the late Sir James Luttrell in Somerset and Devon specifically excepted. The King, moreover, appointed Philip Beaumont esquire to be Constable of Dunster

Castle and steward of all the lordships and lands that went with it. In 1472 King Edward IV appointed a certain Robert Gogh to be bailiff of Dunster and keeper of Marshwood Park, Luttrell's other property in the Hundred of Carhampton.

In December 1472 Lady Herbert, mother of William Herbert, succeeded in obtaining a grant entitling her to keep the Honour of Dunster and other possessions of the late Sir James Luttrell at an annual rent of £90. Heartbroken, bewildered and dishevelled, she eventually moved into Kentisford Farm, a Luttrell property near Blue Anchor Bay, later sold to the Wyndham family. Kentisford Farm is close to Watchet, opposite Five Bells and next to Jenny Cridland's Copse and West Somerset Railway.

Another example of past meeting present. Lady Elizabeth had in the earlier months of her widowhood been allowed to receive the lands that had been settled on her. When the King's officers took possession of them she lodged a complaint protesting that she was a loyal subject of the reigning monarch, Edward IV. Why did she make that statement? Certainly she would do all she could to protect her interests and those of her children, but her husband, Sir James Luttrell, had been found guilty of killing Edward's father, the Duke of York on the field of battle. After a judicial enquiry the King's commissioners were found to be acting lawfully, therefore Elizabeth had to remain outside Dunster Castle's estates.

Kentisford Farm, Watchet, where Elizabeth Luttrell lived with her children. The mill leat in the foreground runs just south of Washford River.

After Elizabeth's departure from the castle, the Earl of Pembroke declared that the running of the estates had been lax in past times and introduced stricter controls on the whole borough. In April 1467 he stipulated:

...that nobody henceforth shall put dung, straw, or other nuisances in the water running to the lord's mills at any time of the week. That nobody shall make linen cloth of 'flockys', and if it be proven by anyone that then the cloth so made shall be forfeited to the lord (ie himself).

That nobody shall carry swords or lances or other offensible and unlawful arms, contrary to the statute of the King in this respect, and no one shall henceforth shoot with his bows and arrows in the churchyard of Dunster under pain of 40d and no one in the borough shall play dice or cards fined 6s 8d.

Grief-stricken as Elizabeth Luttrell may have been, she soon got married for a second time, to her husband's cousin, Sir Humphrey Audley, brother of Lord Audley. At the Battle of Tewkesbury, Sir Humphrey was taken prisoner and summarily executed on the field of battle. When this tragic news reached her, other bad news was coming in regarding the Courtenays' fortunes in the wars. Beside herself with grief, Elizabeth could do nothing but concentrate on bringing up her young family as best she could.

During the Wars of the Roses the senior branches of the Courtenay family, including Elizabeth's four brothers, adhered to the House of Lancaster, just like the Luttrells. Thomas Courtenay, 6th Earl of Devon, was captured, attainted (i.e. his titles forfeited) and beheaded after the battle of Towton near York in 1461. His younger brother, Sir Henry of Topsham, regained some of the estates, but was debarred from inheriting the title due to the attainder, and was himself beheaded for treason in 1467, while the youngest brother, John, who was restored to the Earldom in 1470, was killed at the battle of Tewkesbury in 1471. This was the end of the senior line. It was also the time of Caxton's printing press when he printed the very first book in English, Chaucer's Canterbury Tales.

Nevertheless the resourceful Lady Elizabeth eventually married a third husband, Thomas Mallet of Enmore on the Quantocks in Somerset. However, according to common medieval custom, she retained the surname of Luttrell until her death in the reign of Henry VII. It was under that name that she, in 1476, stood godmother to Richard, the short-lived son of her patron, George, Duke of Clarence. Her feelings at the christening must have been mixed, for it was performed at Tewkesbury, the very place where her late husband had lost his head. With the help of Clarence she eventually repossessed Dunster Castle and all estates bequeathed to her by her first husband.

So Elizabeth had outlived three husbands and suffered persecution and eviction, bereavement and destitution with the loss of all her estates, yet she survived and even outwitted her own son Hugh in a claim he brought against her regarding jewels, plate and household stuff she held in jointure. She retained Court House, where she died in 1493, one year after Columbus discovered the Americas.

Elizabeth Luttrell doing her embroidery at Dunster Castle in more peaceful times

Elizabeth's tomb at Dunster Church

She also paid money for Minehead's new Quay, built in the mid-fifteenth century near the end of today's Blenheim Road, by Lamb Cottage and Beach House.

Lady Luttrell was buried before the high altar in Dunster Church. An incised stone alabaster slab (an expensive kind of limestone marble), which has since been moved to the south aisle of the chancel, shows her attired in a sideless dress faced with ermine, with a mantle lined with ermine, the neck bare, and the head covered with a veil falling below the shoulders. Two angels support a pillow, and there is the usual dog at her feet. The inscription around the slab translates:

Pray, I beseech you, for the soul of Dame Elizabeth Luttrell, who died on the first day of the month of September in the year of our Lord 1493. Now, O Christ, we pray thee have mercy, and do not condemn the redeemed whom thou camest to redeem when lost.

It appears that the tombstone of this illustrious lady was regarded with little or no respect during the years when the Priory church was regarded as simply a burial ground for the Luttrell family. It was neglected and uncared for until the Victorian Luttrells, aided by Amelia Anne Hood, put matters to rights during the great restoration of the Church in the 1870s.

CHAPTER 4

DAME MARGARET WYNDHAM

1500-1580

Dame Margaret earns her place among our notable ladies of Dunster because, although she was certainly quarrelsome, she was interested only in her son George Luttrell's welfare and the Luttrell estates, guarding them against the 'miserly lawyer' Hugh Stewkely from Marsh. Luttrell's wardship had been sold by the Crown to Stewkeley, a shady lawyer who took advantage of his youth and inheritance to offer George, at the age of just 15, the choice of his two daughters. The tithe receipts and the responsibility for appointing a vicar were also conveyed to him. Dame Margaret, in 1556, accused him, amongst many other things, of not making proper provision for a curate, although he was receiving a healthy tithe income; miserly indeed.

Dame Margaret Wyndham, d.1580 (unknown British artist). Portrait in Inner Hall

Dame Margaret was the daughter of Thomas Wyndham, of Felbrigg in Norfolk. She married Andrew Luttrell of Dunster Castle in 1514 and was the mother of Sir John Luttrell, whose famous portrait hangs in Inner Hall. Dame Margaret's portrait is on adjacent wall and the inscriptions reads 'AN 1562 aged 62'. She is depicted in a tight black bodice and white ruff.

The Luttrells were naturally opposed to this union between Andrew Luttrell and 'a slut and [of] no good qualities' and Dame Margaret, 'his grandmother, threatened to prevent him from succeeding to Dunster priory. The marriage took place within two months of his grandmother's death. Stukeley made strong rent demands against his son-in-law as soon as he came of age.

It was Dame Margaret's vehement opposition to her grandson George Luttrell's choice of bride, Joan Stewkely, that caused so much trouble for the bride and groom. She stated that if George married Joan she would 'cast him away' and make him a 'poor gentleman' for marrying the daughter of a miserly lawyer who had constantly opposed the Luttrells in the past. However, in her will dated March 1580 she bequeathed to him the hanging arras or woven tapestry that had been specially made for the parlour at Dunster, two bowls of silver gilt, a drinking cup of silver gilt that had belonged to his father, Thomas Luttrell, two spoons and a salt, along with the Priory of Dunster, which she had previously purchased with all the lands and profits belonging to it.

Dame Margaret had a very considerable income from the estates settled on her as a widow. She invested some of her savings in the purchase of the Priory of Dunster after the Dissolution in 1536, thereby saving the Benedictine church of St George from destruction and also consolidating the properties for her children. In 1543 she was registered as the owner of a ship of 100 tons belonging to the port of Minehead, but at that time berthed in London. This may have been the very ship that her son, Sir John Luttrell, equipped for his intended ill-fated voyage to Africa's Gold Coast with his uncle Thomas Wyndham and the great explorer Sebastian Cabot, some eight years later.

Dame Margaret lived to a great age, surviving her husband by more than forty years. She was a very strong-willed lady and enjoyed the rights to both East Quantoxhead and Marshwood Park, which were both enclosed by a ditch and pale with one hundred deer in each. The deer from Marshwood would eventually be moved to Dunster and Henry Fownes Luttrell's new deer park, driven by Farmer Herne of Carhampton, whose portrait is in the Morning Room (Man holding a Fish).

Margaret died in 1580, and her tomb and that of her husband Sir Andrew Luttrell can be seen in the church at Court House. She left four sons and four daughters, each to have a fortune of 400 marks at age eighteen and twenty-one respectively. Sir John Luttrell, her eldest son, was to receive in addition his father's raiment and all his bows and arrows.

The Wyndham family are descended from Sir John Wyndham (1443–1503) and his wife Margaret (1443–1524), daughter of John Howard, Duke of Norfolk, a direct descendant of Edward I. Succeeding generations have played an important role in English politics, the law, the military and the arts.

Branches of the family are styled variously as Earl of Egremont, Earl of Thomond and Baron Ibracken, Baron

Wyndham, Baron Leconfield and Baron Egremont, Wyndham baronets of Trent, Wyndham baronets of Pilsden Court, and Wyndham baronets of Orchard Wyndham. The senior line of the Wyndham family is today represented by Max Wyndham, Baron Egremont, who lives at the family seat of Petworth House in Sussex.

CHAPTER 5

CATHERINE LUTTRELL

(Born 1537, living in 1603)

Catherine Luttrell was the eldest of Sir John Luttrell's three daughters. Her mother, Mary, had been accused of adultery by Sir John himself. Catherine's husband became a Roman Catholic in 1563 and was imprisoned and fined for this in 1568. They both fled abroad in 1570 and Queen Elizabeth seized their goods and confiscated most of his estates. Lady Catherine was allowed to return to England but Sir Thomas died in exile.

Elizabethan England remains a place and a time that fascinates us, so much so that radio, television and cinema are awash with the Tudor age and the English renaissance. Like other periods in English history, the Luttrell family have their own story to tell in the history of the nation's affairs. Catherine Luttrell's life was caught up in the intrigues and religious conflicts in which King Edward VI,

Queen Mary I (Bloody Mary), Queen Elizabeth I, Mary, Queen of the Scots and King Phillip of Spain loomed large as the political and religious protagonists of the period.

Catherine's father, Sir John Luttrell, had more than his fair share of involvement and conflict during the Tudor period. If walls could talk, then the remains of the Tudor stonework at Dunster Castle would have some tales to tell.

Henry VIII and his fourth wife Anne of Cleeves, who once had Catherine Luttrell and her maternal grandmother Margaret Edgcombe serve for her.

It is worth mentioning the immediate Tudor connections at this early stage. A mere twenty years previously, Sir John Luttrell had been one of the chief English commissioners sent to negotiate with the Scots in March 1549 in order to bring about Henry VIII's desire that the two kingdoms be united by the marriage of Mary, Queen of the Scots and the young Prince Edward VI. Her grandmother,

Dame Margaret Wyndham (portrait in Inner Hall) had saved the Benedictine Priory of St George at Dunster from destruction at the dissolution of the monasteries by buying the actual Priory.

Catherine Luttrell had served in the Household of Queen Mary (Bloody Mary) in the Queen's privy chamber. Both Catherine and her maternal grandmother, Catherine Edgecombe (portrait in King Charles Room), had previously served in the household of Anne of Cleves, Henry VIII's fourth wife, whose marriage had been annulled in July 1540 on the grounds that it had never been consummated after seven months. Anne of Cleves had been portrayed as being kind, fun loving, a bit naive, but not that attractive.

It has been stated that Henry referred to Anne as a "Flanders Mare", which may or may not be true; nevertheless, the label has stuck. Her pre-contract of marriage with Francis I, Duke of Lorraine, was cited as grounds for an annulment. Anne agreed to this, claiming that the marriage had not been consummated, and because she had not resisted the annulment, she was given a generous settlement, including Hever Castle, former home of Henry's former in-laws, the Boleyns. She was given the name "the King's Sister", and became a friend to him and his children until his death. Although she only lived to the age of 41, she outlived both the King and his last two wives, making her the last of the six wives to die.

Catherine Luttrell's mother, Mary Rice, was accused of adultery by her father, Sir John Luttrell, who had been captured, taken prisoner in Scotland and ransomed. With Catherine's change of religion in the age of persecution, the forfeiture of her estates and imprisonment, a life was a chequered one indeed. Added to this was the fact that her husband, Thomas Copley, or Lord Copley to his contemporaries, was one of the chief Roman Catholic exiles in the reign of Elizabeth I, with the eldest of his four sons, Henry, becoming a Jesuit priest. In 1572, when Henry was staying with the Copleys, his uncle Thomas Copley, already out of favour with Queen Elizabeth both for being a Catholic and for having jilted her cousin in favour of the young and beautiful Catherine Luttrell, suddenly took his family into exile. It was decided that Henry, when he was 15, should follow them, to complete his studies at the Jesuit school in Douai, France.

Catherine Luttrell had served in the household of Queen Mary (Bloody Mary) in the queen's privy chamber. Both Catherine and her maternal grandmother, Catherine Edgecombe (portrait in King Charles Room) had previously served in the household of Anne of Cleeves, and under the will of Dame Catherine Edgcumbe, Catherine Luttrell, aged fourteen, received a chain of gold with a flower set with two diamonds and a ruby. After Sir John's death from the 'Sweating Sickness' in 1551, the Earl of Arundel purchased the wardship of Catherine for 100 marks. Soon after, in March 1557, the Earl was awarded custody of the other two daughters, Dorothy and Mary, with an annuity backdated to the time of Sir John's death.

Thomas Copley was rich and highly connected. He was

related to the ill-fated Anne Boleyn through his great-grandfather, Sir Roger Copley, whose daughter Jane, married Sir Geoffrey Boleyn, and was the great-grandmother of Anne Boleyn. Thomas Copley sat in several Parliaments, and the Queen Elizabeth herself stood godmother to their eldest son in 1561. He too, was then a zealous protestant, and was much in favour with his kinswoman Queen Elizabeth at the commencement of her reign.

Maxwell Lyte refers to the wedding and the curious letter from Thomas Copley to the Master of the Revels, a notable Protestant, asking for the loan of a mask at the wedding for, presumably, the banquet held afterwards. We hear more of this story from P. W. Hasler, who tried to shed light on the matter as Thomas Copley had written beforehand to his friend Sir Thomas Cawarden, Master of the Revels, on July 18th that he (Copley) had married a Catholic and for Cawarden '...*secretly to lend me the use of one of your masks for one night against this my marriage which (in an ill hour to me) is like to be solemnized on Sunday next at Nonsuch*, where my hope is I shall see you, and so I do most heartily require you I may do. My hope is there shall no harm come of it'.*

If this was not merely humorous, it may mean that the Queen intended to be present and that Copley did not relish the prospect of being seen by her; Catherine and Thomas were right in the thick of it on this occasion. Previously Thomas had enjoyed royal favour during Elizabeth's reign until his conversion to Catholicism. He sat for the same place in the later parliaments of 1556, 1557, 1559, and 1563, and distinguished himself in 1558 by his opposition to the government of Philip and Mary (Commons' Journals). Queen Mary I of England, a Catholic queen, had died in 1558 and was succeeded by her half-sister, Elizabeth, a protestant.

At first the authorities ignored the matter. He returned himself once more for Gatton to the Parliament of 1563 and was re-appointed to the commission of the peace in 1564. His attitude towards the established church was not noticed (favourably or unfavourably) in the report made by the bishop of his diocese to the Privy Council in that year. But in 1568 Thomas Copley was imprisoned and fined for materially helping the English Catholic exiles at Louvain. Next, in November 1569, his office of JP necessitated his taking the oath required by the Acts of Supremacy and Uniformity. 'I cannot yet,' he wrote to the sheriff, 'by any search, find sufficient matter to persuade me with safe conscience to that which is at present required of me'.

It is also worth noting that Mary, Queen of the Scots, Elizabeth's cousin, was the Catholic heiress to Scotland's throne. While not mentioned in Henry VIII's succession will, the strikingly beautiful princess was related to the Tudor line and had some claim to the throne. Although most English Catholics recognized Elizabeth's rule, the Catholic world officially denied the legality of Henry VIII's marriage to Anne Boleyn, since they did not recognize the annulment of his marriage to Catherine of Aragon.

In 1586 letters sent to Mary, Queen of Scots by a

Catholic called Anthony Babington were found. The letters revealed a plot to kill Elizabeth and replace her with Mary. This became known as the infamous Babington Plot. Elizabeth had no choice but to sign Mary's death warrant. Mary Queen of Scots was beheaded at Fotheringay Castle on February 8th 1587. Babington was a young Catholic noble who joined the plot to depose the Protestant Queen Elizabeth I and put Mary, Queen of Scots, a Catholic, on the English throne. The History of Parliament: Gatton Borough claims Catherine Luttrell was involved in this plot and states the following:

Thomas Copley's widow, (Catherine Luttrell) who does not appear to have taken any interest in parliamentary patronage at Gatton, became involved in the Babington plot. Sir Francis Walsingham wrote to three of his friends in the county, Sir Thomas Brown, and Richard Bostock that... whereas my lords of the council do understand that Mistress Copley hath the nomination of the two burgesses for the town of Gatton, being a parcel of her jointure, it is not thought convenient, for that she is known to be evil affected, that she should bear any sway in the choice of the said burgesses.

The execution of Mary, Queen of Scots was the final insult to King Phillip of Spain. In having her cousin executed Elizabeth had just killed the next heir, who was a Catholic, and she had also made deals with countries who were Philip's enemies. On top of this Sir Francis Drake (who was in effect a pirate) had stolen much of the gold and riches that Spain had taken from America. Hence in 1588, the year after the tragic and ill-fated Mary was beheaded, he launched his Armada against England.

Margaret Edgcombe, grandmother to Catherine Luttrell. Portrait in King Charles Room, Dunster Castle, by an artist of the British (English) School. National Trust.

In her lifetime Catherine Luttrell was described as "simple" and unfit to meddle with politics, but being a noted bigot she was regarded with suspicion, and was committed to prison once if not twice in her later years. She was living in 1603. Little was she to know that 300 years later, in 1931, Dunster Castle was to play host to an Elizabethan Fayre & Maske with Geoffrey Luttrell playing the part of King Henry VIII and the Rt Hon Maud Ackland Hood as Anne Boleyn.

Thomas Copley died in Flanders in 1584, and in the last codicil to his will he styled himself "Sir Thomas Copley, knight, Lord Copley of Gatton in the county of Surrey". By his wife Catherine, daughter and coheiress of Sir John Luttrell of Dunster, Somerset, he had four sons and four daughters. One of the sons, Henry Copley, was Queen Elizabeth's godson. He died young and features in the allegorical painting. Mary, his third daughter, was nine years old at the time of Sir Thomas's death. She married Henry Shelley of Mapledurham in Hampshire, who was a cousin of Thomas Copley and also an English Catholic Recusant.

Every picture tells a story, and the enigmatic memorial of Thomas Copley and Catherine Luttrell is no exception. The oil painting which now hangs in the Inner Hall was bought by George Luttrell in 1906. This is one of the Dunster Castle's more obscure and largely unsung paintings, yet the story of their lives together took place during a time historians now consider to be the golden age of English history, one of secrecy, intrigue and treason. In this picture, Sir Thomas Copley is represented in a tabard bearing the arms of Copley and Hoo quarterly, kneeling at a faldstool, with his five sons behind him. On the opposite side, Lady Copley is represented in a mantle bearing the arms of Luttrell and Ryce alternately, similarly kneeling and attended by her four daughters.

South Front, Nonsuch Palace, Surrey. Built by King Henry VIII in 1538 during the Dissolution of the Monasteries, this palace was considered to be one of the finest architectural wonders of the world. 'Nonsuch' was named so because there was no other like it, and it stood for 150 years. Only four pictures were ever painted of it.

The central part of the picture is intended to illustrate the progress of the human soul from earth to heaven. The flesh and the devil endeavour to hold it, but death cuts their gilded cords with his scythe and the soul ascends through thirteen concentric circles representing the Ptolemaic system. In the Empyrean Heaven above is the crucified Saviour attended by Saints, and in the circumference are Seraphim, Cherubim, Thrones, Dominions, Virtues, Powers, Principalities, Archangels and Angels, according

to the Dionysian arrangement which was followed by
Dante and others. This 'device' of Sir Thomas Copley,

A Religious Allegory with Catherine Luttrell and Thomas Copley and Family. The Latin
inscription below the painting reveals his life and times whilst abroad. British (English)
School. Inner Hall, Dunster Castle, National Trust

having been approved by the theologians of the University of Paris in 1580, was engraved there in that year. In 1625 his eldest daughter, Margaret, added a Latin inscription and three coats of arms to the original painting.

Translation of the Latin inscription beneath the allegorical painting of Sir Thomas Copley by Catherine Pooley:

This allegory to illustrate the three English campaigns of Sir Thomas Copley, the Baron of Wells has been cleverly arranged from them and was arranged in 1580 by the theologians of the Paris School. It has not left out his firstborn daughter Joan, the only wife of the remarkable leader Peiridus Martignus Master of the Cavalry in the Franco Belgian (?) The house of Governor Philip has been restored into that better union which it had before, so that to those who may honour this design will speak out from the soul of its dead and noble creator and shall act piously, and so that succeeding generations with this example of the unsullied faithfulness of soldiers always before their eyes will have a memorial. This is deliberately placed here in AD 1625.

The following is from Somerset Heritage Centre to John Robins, volunteer research at Dunster Castle, with reference to Catherine Luttrell, Thomas Copley painting, George Luttrell and Maxwell Lyte:

There are no other letters than the ones you have from Maxwell Lyte dealing with the Sir Thomas Copley in the File at The records Office. I have therefore completed the letter of the 15th – including the gaps and put in Italics something, which may be of interest. I have retyped the entire letter of the 24th May, which gives George Mackay's address. Letter of 21st.May revealed nothing extra. There were also 3 letters from George Mackay to George Luttrell in 1907. One mentions the painting and I have typed it below.

Source: Somerset Records Office.
Luttrell Files. Ref . No. DD/L Box 196, - Tin Box B/3

Allegorical Painting of Sir Thomas Copley
(Inner Hall, Dunster Castle)
Letter from Maxwell Lyte to Uncle George
(George Fownes Luttrell)
15th. May 1906.

Dear Uncle George,
Catherine, eldest daughter and co heiress of Sir John Luttrell married Sir Thomas Copley of Sutton in Surrey. She did not inherit Dunster because her father left his funds to his brother Thomas who bought out such rights as she had. Her husband is an interesting person and sat in several parliaments.

Queen Elizabeth stood Godmother to their eldest son but Copley had turned Norman Catholic and took service under Phillip II in the Netherlands and he was recognised as leader of the Irish Romanists abroad. He claimed to be Lord Hoo, Lord Welles and even Lord Copley in England as he was created a Baron by Phillip II. One of his sons became distinguished among the Jesuits.

A dealer in curiosities of Birmingham has sent up for my inspection a very curious emblematical picture devised by Sir Thomas Copley in 1580, and afterwards somewhat altered in 1625 by his eldest daughter who was married in Flanders. It represents the passage of the souls from Earth to Heaven through concentric circles after the Ptolemaic system. have not yet ascertained how far this agrees with Dante or Milton. The flesh and the Devil hold a cord which death is cutting with a scythe. Around this are cherubims, seraphims, archangels etc. not in this order. Derived from Dionysius.

Below Sir Copley, in a tabard bearing the Arms of Copley and Hoo, kneels at a footstool. Behind him are his five sons, opposite at another footstool kneels his wife in a mantle bearing the Arms of Luttrell and Ryce who was her mother. Behind her are her four daughters. The Luttrell Arms appears in two other parts of the picture. There is a long Latin explanation, explanatory inscription. The picture is about a yard high. It wants a new strainer and a simple frame and a coat of varnish but it is otherwise in fair condition, Aunt Annie has seen it and I hope to show it to May. It is a curious coincidence that there should be an allegorical picture of this sort devised by the son-in-law of de Heere's subject. Of course it's not beautiful but it is extremely interesting. I think it was painted for a domestic chapel and I hope shortly to find out when it was brought over to England.

In the meantime I give these particulars as you may wish to buy it. The man wishes 12 guineas for it, which appears to me reasonable, as it does not fall into any ordinary category of picture.

PS.

I have mentioned the picture in my new chapter about Sir John Luttrell and shall expand my notice of it if you buy it. May has seen it this morning. If it related to one of my ancestors I should buy it without hesitation

24th May 1906.
From Maxwell Lytte
Dear Uncle George,
I had quite thought that I had enclosed Mr Mackay's letter and I cannot find it now, everything here being turned upside down for an evening party on Tuesday.

It was to the effect that a loss of £2.2s on the price asked was nothing to him in comparison with the pleasure of knowing that the picture could henceforth be in the proper place. He also expressed a hope that if he were in the neighbourhood of Dunster, you would allow him to see it again. If the letter turns up, I will forward it. In the meantime I write to say that the writer is:

George Mackay,
70, New Street,
Birmingham.

There are three letters from George Mackay to George Luttrell dealing with a portrait of one of the Mrs Luttrells. In one of the letters, dated 5th October 1907, Mackay says, "My kind regards to Sir Thomas Copley. I suppose he is still such fun".

CHAPTER 6

THE WARRIOR LADY AND THE SIEGE OF DUNSTER

Jane Luttrell, ??-1668

The English Civil War at Dunster

Women have been involved in wars throughout history, whether they carry a gun or excite men's desire, either of which being just as deadly. Their looks and beauty have always been among their most powerful weapons.

Lady Jane Luttrell, husband of Sir Thomas, was without doubt the most determined and warlike of all the women of Dunster. She was a staunch Parliamentary defender of the castle during the English Civil War in 1643, and she sent the Royalist army running for their lives in August of that year. She thoroughly deserves her place in the castle's hall of fame.

Jane was the daughter of Sir Francis Popham of Littlecote in Wiltshire, an active politician and noted Parliamentarian. The arms of Luttrell impaled by those of Popham may be seen at Marshwood, Blue Anchor, and it is probable that they lived there until the death of her father in 1629.

Jane Luttrell orders the castle garrison to open fire on the Royalists. Illustration by Peter Stevenson, NT 1997

Marshwood House, where the façade can be clearly seen from the A39 road going north after village of Washford. Marshwood has recently been given a complete makeover, but the entrance porch and fenestrations are 16th century.

In the spring and summer of 1640, Thomas Luttrell was one of only three Somerset deputy lieutenants who actively mobilized soldiers to serve in the Second Bishops' War, or as Jane would have known it, Bellum Episcopale, which was a prelude to the carnage that was to follow. This second brief war was between Charles I of England and the Scots. Charles summoned Parliament in order to raise an army against the Scots, who invaded northern England, won a battle at Newburn on the Tyne (28 August 1640), and occupied Northumberland and Durham. The war was ended by the Treaty of Ripon (26 October 1640), which forced Charles to summon the Long Parliament, which in turn led to the English Civil War.

At the very outset of the Civil War in August 1642, the Earl of Bedford, commanding for the Parliament, at once issued warrants for the apprehension of any of the Royalist party and sent off posts to Thomas Luttrell, bidding him strengthen and make good his castle at Dunster. This order was promptly obeyed, and Thomas Luttrell and his wife, increased their garrison by a hundred men, also adding more cannons. Anticipating moreover that the Royalists would endeavour to cross over to Wales, Lady Jane sent a troop of soldiers to disable or remove the rudders from all ships berthed in Minehead harbour, including coal ships and fishing vessels.

The Royalist Lord Hertford duly arrived in Minehead and fortified himself in a "strong Inn", and then, under his Lieutenant General, Sir Ralph Hopton, rode to Dunster and attempted to gain possession of Dunster Castle, barely two miles away. Sixty Cavaliers were sent there to demand entry on pain of death, a demand that was immediately and forcefully denied. After a brief conversation and further attempts to gain entry, "Mistresse" Luttrell commanded her soldiers within to "give fire". The Royalist officer told the castle's defenders not to obey this order, but Jane Luttrell, now furious, again commanded them "upon their very lives to do it", which they did with purpose and vengeance.

To be fired upon from behind strong castle ramparts was more than these cavaliers expected, or could withstand, so they suddenly wheeled around and beat a hasty retreat back to Minehead. The first shots in West Somerset had now been fired by forces for Parliament manning Dunster Castle under the command of Jane Luttrell.

Although the Royalist infantry eventually managed to escape in some coal ships from Porlock to Wales, the inhabitants of both Minehead and Dunster were fearful of them returning by surprise and gaining possession of the castle "from which it was considered that 10,000 men would not be able to dislodge them". The King's cavalry went further westward and into Devon.

Around this time in August, so a contemporary story states, a massive storm with loud claps of thunder and dazzling lightning had been brewing over the Bristol Channel and a Royalist ship from Wales, attempting to berth in Minehead harbour, had been driven east onto rocks at Blue Anchor Bay, floundering on the ebb tide. This was probably witnessed by the Parliamentary garrison stationed on the castle's north-eastern battlements.

Jane was quick to react, and she sent a troop of horse to investigate. On arrival they found the vessel completely beached, and were fired upon by the Royalists as they made their way towards the ship in the soft sand. The

Parliamentarians returned fire and after a brief skirmish they seized the vessel, which was evidently carrying provisions, muskets, rifles and ammunition for the royalists based in Minehead. This was the first time in British history that cavalry had managed to capture a hostile man o'war at sea, and it was on Jane's watch.

Early in January 1643, a group of Welsh managed to blockade Minehead Harbour, preventing the entry of any boats or ships. The siege stopped the supply of essential provisions as well as coal. Under Captain Paulet another five hundred Welshmen or so landed and immediately seized the town of Minehead and surrounding area.

Paulet was later accused of, "constraining the inhabitants to yield to any taxation and to submit themselves servants and slaves to save their throats from being cut."

Captain Paulet then attacked Dunster Castle, but Thomas and Jane Luttrell, being prepared, were able to repel them and save the town from plunder and worse. A shot rang out from the castle, followed by cannon fire that killed some Royalist soldiers. Captain Paulet was enraged, and vowed to quarter the murderer and hang his limbs from the battlements as food for ravens. In fact Paulet moved onto Barnstaple with two hundred musketeers and forty horsemen.

Jane's fortunes soon began to change. In June 1643 her husband was persuaded to hand over the castle to his cousin, the Royalist Col Wyndham, as Charles was winning the war in Somerset. Within a few days of the

Thomas Luttrell (1584-1644) husband of Jane: English School of Painters.
Portrait in the Inner Hall, Dunster Castle (National Trust)

death of Thomas Luttrell in February 1644 Jane, who was
now back at Marshwood in Blue Anchor, was compelled

to pay a large sum to the Crown, as appears by the following receipt:

13th February 1643. Then received of Mrs Jane Luttrell the summe of fiveteene hundred pounds, as soe much due to his Majestie for the fyne of her selfe and her two sonnes; I say received for his Majestie's service the day and yeere (sic) above written the summe of 1500, by me Francis Hawley.

The person who gave it was merely an officer in the Royalist army, but the payment might possibly be regarded as the purchase money for the wardship of the heir of the Dunster estate, who was a minor at the time of his father's death.

A few weeks later, there is another acquittance:

25 to die Marcii 1644, anno regni Regis Caroli 19o. Receaved then of Mistriss Jane Luttrell the summe of three score pownds in parte of payment of one hundred pownds which she was to pay by way of loane upon His Majestie's lettre in the nature of a privie seale for His Majestie's service. I say receaved. Per me William Prowse, deput' vicecomitis.

Jane Luttrell must have been loath indeed to furnish money for the party which she and her relations had so steadily opposed. In later and happier times, she continued to live at Marshwood, where she hoarded her savings, of which she was later robbed. Jane died in 1668 and now lies in Dunster Church.

CHAPTER 7

THE EXTRAVAGANCE OF MARY TREGONWELL

Debtors, Creditors and Disasters

Meet the beautiful Mary Tregonwell, a lady who was as wealthy – and free with her money - as she was beguiling. Mary's story is set against the struggle between the Catholic King James II, James, Duke of Monmouth, the Prince William of Orange and his 'Glorious Revolution'.

William's invasion consisted of some 250 ships which anchored in Torbay, Devon in November 1688. William of Orange with his Protestant army landed to press his wife Mary's own claim to the throne.

Mary Stuart was the daughter of King James II and had married William of Orange, but this pushed her claim into second place as James's wife, Mary of Modena, had a son. When William left Torbay and landed in London, King

Mary Tregonwell

James fled to France. As a result Parliament agreed that James had vacated his throne and offered the Crown to William and Mary.

Heiress of John Tregonwell, of Milton Abbas in Dorset, Mary Tregonwell was born in 1642 at Milton Abbas, just north of the National Trust property of Kingston Lacy. Her mother was the daughter of a former Mayor of London. Her great grandfather, Sir John Tregonwell, was a lawyer who had helped arrange King Henry VIII's divorce from Catherine of Aragon, and at the Dissolution of the Monasteries he acted as a commissioner receiving the surrender of the many and varied abbeys. He had bought Milton Abbas in 1540 for £1,000 and converted it into a private mansion. He died in 1565, but the Tregonwell family continued at Milton Abbey for more than a century afterwards. Mary inherited the house in 1680 and on the 15th July that same year she married Col. Francis Luttrell of Dunster Castle.

In November 1688 Col Francis Luttrell was one of the most important men called upon by Prince William of Orange to raise an independent company of foot soldiers. He applied himself to the task with such energy that he collected the necessary men in three days and maintained them at his own expense. The local tradesman, however,

Raising of the Green Howards, 1688, by Terence Cuneo 1985

took advantage of this haste and charged him £1,500 for uniforms and clothes 'that soon proved worthless'. The regiment, however, was of more enduring quality and is still in existence today, known as The Green Howards and amalgamated with Yorkshire 1 Battalion.

Mary Tregonwell was noted as an intelligent woman and beloved by all. She had an independent income of £2,500, the capital value of which she herself estimated as £50,000. She spent incredible sums of money on buying trendy clothes for herself and her husband, their children and servants. Mary had many jewels, one of which was reported to be worth £800, a great sum in those days. She had a fine diamond necklace with a picture of her husband set in gold with diamonds round it, and a 'crossiatt' of diamonds. We have her to thank for providing the funds for the commissioning of the Grand Staircase and ceiling, the dining room and servery ceilings at Dunster Castle.

Other examples of her London spending include this impressive list:

A morning gown, £4 12s.

A Venetian morning gown lined with blue satin, cap and sleepers, £7

A set of sterling plate buttons, £5

A gold sword, £3 7s

A rich gold necklcloth, £1 1s 6d

2 pair of Doeskin gloves, 6s Trimming them and facing, 3s

3 pairs of perfumed gloves, 15s 6d

A black French hat edged with gold, and a gold hat-band 17s.

Franklyn, their London suppliers, began to increase their goods at the birth of Mary's eldest daughter. The following are some of the items:

1681, October 10: A suite of lace childbed linen, mantle and apron, £10. Broad fine lace, £6 10s. 7 yards broad fine lace, 30s per yard, £10 10s. 6 yards of broad fine lace att (sic) 22s per yard £6 10s.

> *A bone lace night raile, £6 6s. A cornet and coife, £6. 5s.*
> *A childbed suite of fine Holland, £1. A pair of bone lace ruffles, £2.*
> *A silver porringer and spoone, £1. 5s.*
> *Another suite of fine lace linen, £6 10s.*
> *Damask and diaper for clouts, £12 15s.*
> *A rich gold fringe for petticoat, £12 10s.*

Eventually Mary Luttrell's debts to William Franklyn amounted to £819 13s 8d, of which £15 10s 6d represented interest on £345 for nine months. A good part of the items on the bills were for clothes for her children. Thus we find the following:

1683, March 17: A crimson and white silk coate for Master, £1. 18s

May 2:, Making a greene silk coate for Master, 8s. 4 yards of rich Italian silk at 11s per yard, £2 4s.

August 22: Paid for making 2 silver coates, 31 4s. 10 yards of rich gold and silver silke for both coates, at 33s per yard, £16 18s 4d

1987, April 2nd: Making of 3 velvet coates for the children, £1 15s. 24 yards strip(ped) scarlett velvet, at 16s 6d £19 16s. 9 yards scarlett strip(ped) sik to face them, at 5s 6d, £2 9s 6d.

Mary, her son Tregonwell Luttrell and father Frances Luttrell descend the Grand
Staircase at Dunster Castle (NT cartoon, Peter Stevenson)

Unfortunately, Francis' untimely death in 1690 gave rise
to a good deal of trouble and meant that Mary would need
every penny of her wealth. Unconsciously, or regardless of
the condition of her husbands' affairs, she had his body
removed to St George's Church, Dunster, for interment,
and spent the then considerable sum of £300 on his
funeral.

Colonel Francis Luttrell

She was soon forced to contest in the Court of Canterbury against Alexander Luttrell, younger brother of Francis. Alexander was the guardian of her three children, who were all under age. It was not until 1693 that Mary and the executors undertook the administration of the estate.

Trouble soon began, with creditors making their voices

heard. The debts had amounted to £12,000 in addition to a sum of £10,000 due to Alexander Luttrell. One loan, of £4,000 from a Luttrell cousin, Sir William Wyndham, was secured upon the manor of Beggarhuish and other lands, part of the ancient inheritance of the Luttrells of East Quantoxhead, so these all passed away from the family. The debts secured by judgement came next, but there were various creditors who stood to lose heavily, the bulk of the real property being strictly predetermined. Servants' wages had not been paid for years. Mary had a jointure of £1,500 per year which she would not forego. Several members of the Dyke family who had a claim upon her late husband's personal estate retaliated by contending that her expensive jewels should be considered part of the estate.

Under her husband's will Mary was entitled to a life-interest in all his furniture, of which she had purchased many pieces herself, so she probably used some of her own money to rescue it from her creditors. The fate of other belongings is recorded by Narcissus Luttrell, a literary figure from Chelsea and a distant descendant of the Luttrells of Dunster. He was also a historian, diarist, and bibliographer, and briefly Member of Parliament for two different Cornish boroughs. Under the date of 19th November 1696 he wrote:

Yesterday morning a sudden fire happened in Mrs Luttrell's house in St James's Street, being newly and richly furnished, which burnt it to the ground, the lady herself narrowly escaping, and 'tis said she lost plate, jewells, &c. to the value of £10,000.

Just a few weeks after this catastrophe, we find Mary marrying Jacob Bancks, who was Swedish by birth but held a commission as Captain in the English Navy. He was a Swedish naval officer born in Stockholm who came to England in 1681 as a diplomat. According to one story, it was he who rescued Mary from the flames. Had he been staying overnight? Although the Swede had secured the hand of an English heiress, he clearly was not proficient in writing her native language. It may be noted by the way that he did not marry again. Milton Abbess eventually passed to his second son and from him to a cousin, a foreigner who was in no way related to the father of Lady Bancks.

Jacob Bancks was knighted in 1699 and, through the Luttrell influence, was elected to represent Minehead in nine successive Parliaments. Mary Tregonwell, now Lady Bancks, died of smallpox on the 2nd March 1704 exactly two years after Queen Ann ascended the throne. She was buried at the family home of Milton Abbas, where there is a monument to her memory.

Mary and Francis had four children, a son, Tregonwell, and three daughters, Mary, Jane and Frances. Milton Abbas eventually passed to second son and from him to a cousin, a foreigner who was in no way related to the father of Lady Bancks.

Mary, born in 1681, was the second child and became entitled to £4,000. She married a widower, Sir George Rooke, a famous admiral, on January 29th 1701. She died in childbirth about 18 months later and was buried at

Hortin in Kent. Queen Anne and Prince George of Denmark stood as godparents to her infant, while Queen Anne and Prince George of Denmark stood as godparents to her first born, Tregonwell.

Another curious twist is that very shortly after Mary's death Sir Jacob Bancks entered into an odd arrangement with Dorothy Luttrell, wife of Col Alexander Luttrell, the details of which come from his own hand:

I doe accnouledge to have received the sum off five guineas to pay Missis Doroty Luttrell the sum of fifty guineas in case I do marie after the 14th day of Agust 1704, in witness thereof I have sett my hand this 14th day Agust 1704 aforesed, J Bancks, A. Fownes.

Mary Banks (Mary Tregonwell) in Milton Abbas church, Dorset

Jacob Bancks is remembered with their son on the tomb chest on which she lies. Bancks Street in Minehead is named after him, while Tregonwell Road is named after Mary.

Alexander Luttrell acquired by marriage the ex-monastic properties of the elder branch of the Tregonwell family in Somerset and Dorset, which were estimated to bring in £2,500 pa. As a Justice of Peace he was hostile to nonconformists. Elected again for Minehead in 1685, he took no known part in James II's Parliament, but he was probably a court supporter. During the summer he commanded a militia regiment against the Duke of Monmouth, but was unable to distinguish himself, as most of his men deserted.

Jacob Bancks served at the Battle of Beachy Head in 1690, taking over from the wounded captain. He later commanded several ships, including HMS Cambridge and HMS Phoenix. He was knighted in 1698 whilst captain of the HMS Russell. He became MP for Minehead from 1698 and became involved in the rougher side of the Tory-Whig factional strife. In 1716 he was implicated in the Jacobite conspiracy the Gyllenberg Plot. He and others had in fact raised some £18000 towards the cause.

Le Neve's Pedigree of Lesser Knights states:

Bank, a tradesman in Stockholm as I was informed by Mitford of Bow in Midds. merchant who knew him.

Jacob banks esq' of Milton Abbas= Captain of the Russell man of war in the service of King William Mary d" of John Tregonwell of Milton Abbas com. dorcet. his sole heir relict of

Collonel Francis Lutterell of Dunster Castle Som'set esq.

1698. Naturalized by Act of Parl, not worth a groat as said, dyed. She dyed of smallpox. day of febr.

1 son. John Banks of Milton Abbas com. Dorcet dyed day of March 2 son.

CHAPTER 8

DOROTHY LUTTRELL AND THE NEW CHAPEL

Dorothy Luttrell, ??-1723

Classical Enlightenment

Dorothy was the daughter of Edward Yarde of Churston Ferrers in Devon. Edward Yarde's family had held Churston since marrying the Ferrers heiress in the reign of Edward IV. His father fought for the King in the Civil War, and was fined a total of £530. As Vice-Warden of the Stannaries, Yarde was probably a follower of the Earl of Bath and an opponent of exclusion.

The first of the family to enter Parliament, Yarde was successful for Dartmouth at the second general election of 1679 and again in 1681. In 1685 he was returned for Ashburton, where he commanded the local company of the Stannaries militia, but again he left no trace on the records of Parliament. He was one of the first Devonshire Tories to be removed from office by James II. In November 1688 William of Orange landed within a couple of miles of Churston, but it is not recorded that Yarde joined him. He accepted the Revolution and was restored to the commission of the peace.

His daughter Dorothy married Alexander Luttrell. The Luttrell family were not long-lived – when Alexander died he was only the sixth head of the family in nine generations to live to the age of forty. For twelve years from the death of Colonel Alexander Luttrell, Dorothy his widow managed the Dunster estate on behalf of their eldest son, Alexander. Alexander was the ninth heir to inherit under age, which inevitably threw a great burden on Dorothy, but as we now know, these Dunster ladies were shrewd judges.

One contemporary describes her as ''a very prudent and charitable gentlewoman', another styles her "the great good lady at the Castle" and a third, in 1720, speaks of her adding to her "former just, charitable and pious actions" by paying the debts of her brother-in-law, Colonel Francis Luttrell, still outstanding.

Dorothy was the first Luttrell to instigate changes to the castle's exterior. She made many changes in and around Dunster Castle. Until her time there was only one approach to the Castle. After ascending the direct road from the town to Sir Hugh Luttrell's gateway and passing under its vaulted archway, carriages, horsemen, and pedestrians alike had to turn abruptly to the right through the earlier gateway of Sir Reynold de Mohun, and thence to describe a curve of the left, still ascending, in order to reach the porch on the western façade of the Jacobean mansion.

From first to last the road was exceedingly steep, and the angle between the two gateways was so sharp that great skill was required to drive a carriage safely through them in descending to the town. Tradition (the Legend of Grisel Gris, see Part 2) says that a horse had its brains dashed out there, and minor accidents must have been numerous. Mrs Luttrell therefore made an alternative road branching off to the left opposite to the stables, and winding upwards round the eastern side of the Tor until it reached the level of the south-eastern angle of the Castle. There it ended in a little platform close to the domestic offices. If it was less dignified than the older approach, it was at least considerably safer.

'The New Way', as it was called, directly opposite the castle stables, was finished in 1720, and the trees lining it are very correctly represented as young in Buck's view of Dunster Castle, which was engraved in 1733. To protect it from above, a yew hedge was planted below the eastern front of the Castle, and this hedge has grown since to a height of about 54 feet.

The New Way was barely finished when Dorothy Luttrell began to build a florid chapel projecting from the eastern front of the Castle, partly on the site of an ancient semi-circular tower. This work was executed in 1723 and the following year, at a cost of about £1300 under the direction of Sir James Thornhill, who painted for the interior a huge picture of 'the Lifting up of the Brazen Serpent'. By a will dated in October 1723, Dorothy Luttrell bequeathed £350 for the completion of the Chapel and there is a statement that it was definitely consecrated. A portrait of George Hooper, Bishop of Bath and Wells, still hanging in castle's back oak staircase appears to be the memorial of this event.

The Lifting Up of the Brazen Serpent. Originally hung in Dorothy Luttrell's chapel, then moved to the Grand Staircase before finally hanging in St George's Church in Luttrell's Chapel.

A silver flagon, salver and silver cup with cover are mentioned in 1744 as belonging to the communion table at Dunster Castle's chapel. These are now in use at St Michael the Archangel at Alcombe, having been presented to them by George Luttrell in the 1860s.

Early in the eighteenth century Dorothy Luttrell's son, Alexander, appears to have levelled the ancient keep and converted it into a bowling green. Any relics of the Chapel of St Stephen and other medieval buildings by the de Mohun family that had survived the demolition of Oliver Cromwell in 1650 were then removed. Some traces of a drain on the west side are all that remain. An octagonal summerhouse at the eastern end of the Bowling Green which almost overhangs the inhabited parts of the castle has a leaden pipe-head with the arms and the date of '1727', four years after Dorothy's death. A large mullioned window in it dates from the 15th century. In 1741, this summer house had "a stove grate and huffer, fire shovels, tongs and poker, and four pieces of the hunting chase" and "a mahogany octagonal table and eight leather bottomed chairs with walnut frames". The room beneath it contained "twelve pair of Brasil bowles and three jacks" valued at £2 11s.

At some period between 1705 and 1737, Dorothy or another Luttrell bought or acquired the magnificent leather hangings in the gallery at Dunster Castle. It has to be said that in 1691 there were some "hangings of gilt leather" in Mrs Luttrell's "Closet" though a note in 1705 states that almost all the furnishings of that room had been "sent to London, except the gilt leather sent to Abbey Milton". This was the work of Mary Tregonwell, undertaken one year after the death of her husband, Col Francis Luttrell.

The New Way was just about completed in 1720 when Dorothy began to build a florid chapel projecting from the eastern front of the castle on South Terrace, partly on the site of a medieval semicircular tower. This was under the direction of Sir James Thornhill. Thornhill was a Dorset man who was then reaching the end of his distinguished career as a mural painter, which had included the baroque decorations in St Paul's Cathedral and the famous Painted Hall at Greenwich. Sadly, no visual record was made of the chapel's interior before it was demolished by Anthony Salvin in 1868 to make way for the enormous Drawing

Watercolour drawing of south front. Dorothy's florid chapel is
middle right. J Buckler 1839

Room tower. We do know however that the chapel was
decorated with panelling, pilasters and stucco ordered by
Dorothy and all was painted a stone colour. There were
also painted festoons between the windows resembling the
chapel Thornhill decorated at Wimpole Hall,
Cambridgeshire, now in the care of the National Trust.
Paintings of Dorothy chapel show the outside was faced

with gleaming white Portland stone, contrasting with the original red sandstone work of the rest of the castle.

By a will dated October 1723, Dorothy Luttrell bequeathed £350 for the completion of the Chapel. There is a definite statement that it was eventually consecrated. The following little memorandum in her handwriting, made shortly before her death, must not be taken to indicate a miserly disposition:

There is in the writing closett £2,300 in money, besides a hundred pound in broad pieces and moyders received by leases.

No bank existed at the time where Dorothy could have conveniently deposited this money. Broad pieces were old hammered gold money from the reign of James 1. Moidores were gold coins from Portugal.

They had three children: Alexander, baptised 10th June 1705, Dorothy, baptised 10th May 1707 and Francis, baptised 18th May 1709

Engraving of Dunster Castle by J Ryland, England Illustrated, 1764.
Dorothy Luttrell's beautiful classical castle.

Withycombe Weeke nearby was sold in 1650 to Thomas Cridland, but by 1710 the manor had been dismembered and in 1714 Dorothy Luttrell bought the remaining farm with a share in the mill. In 1718, she purchased for her son the advowson of the church of Minehead standing just below North Hill or Compass Hill as Dorothy and all seamen used to call it

The patronage of Minehead Church was exercised by Bruton Priory, later Abbey, until the Dissolution of the Monasteries in 1536 and William Moggridge. William and Joan sold it in 1717 to Dorothy Luttrell. John Codrington was charged feodary rent to Dunster honor every third year until 1746 or later but before 1777 lordship was acquired by John Fownes Luttrell and descended with Withycombe Hadley. Patronage descended in the Luttrell family with the manor until 1962, when it was transferred to the Bishop of Bath and Wells.

SIR JAMES THORNHILL, DOROTHY LUTTRELL AND THE CHAPEL IN DUNSTER CASTLE 1721 – 1723

(Extracts from) A DOCUMENTARY STUDY
By Jeremy Barker

Sir James Thornhill, born in Dorset in 1675, was the first great English artist of the eighteenth century and in a very real sense the father of the emergent school of English art that his son-in-law, William Hogarth, later championed so effectively. He was

that rare phenomenon in the eighteenth century, the apprentice who rose to the top of the social order. Thus he became Serjeant-Painter and History Painter to the King, Master of the Painter-Stainers Company, Knight and Member of Parliament for his native town, Weymouth and Melcombe Regis. In an age that had hitherto regarded native artists as too inferior to foreign artists to be entrusted with major works, he proved the contrary and displacing the foreigner, winning the contracts to paint the dome of Saint Paul's Cathedral, Hampton Court and Greenwich, to say nothing of the houses of the great up and down the country – Chatsworth, Blenheim, Hanbury Hall and Wimpole, to name but a few.

What is less well known is that Thornhill was also an accomplished architect. His interest here is amply demonstrated, from the beginning of his career to the end. His early sketchbook, now in the British Museum, gives a convincing picture of his keen interest in all aspects of architecture. So too the notebook of his visit to East Anglia and the Netherlands in 1711, and the notebook of his journey to France in 1717 is artistically speaking chiefly concerned with architecture and interior decoration and the drawings in it are to match George Vertue records that:

March 1722... Sir James having carried his point to be Serjeant painter and history painter, and to be knighted, now on all hands declared himself to be opposite all... (the interest of the Surveyors and Officers of the King's works) and by drawing and designing, and demonstrating their ignorance's in ye Art of Building, he would sett himself up against then for the Place of Surveyor or Architect, and in short for all in all. (1)

Moreover it was around this time that he repurchased, redesigned and rebuilt the family from at Thornhill in Dorset, was Mr Styles' architect for Moor Park. (2) and may well have had a hand likewise in the design of the almshouse he built for decrepit mariners in Melcombe Regis (1772), and he may even have had a hand in Sherborne House for Henry Seymour Portman (1720). He later designed the statues on the Clarendon Building in Oxford and his advice was sought on the façade of the Queen's College in the 1730s. In the aftermath of the great fire in Blandford Forum in 1731, it was to Thornhill that people turned for the rebuilding, though his death in 1734 prevented him from doing anything more than preliminary drawings. Clearly, contemporaries regarded him as an accomplished architect (4).

It is not therefore a matter of surprise that Alexander Luttrell's widow, Dorothy, when seeking an architect to build a chapel in Dunster castle in Somerset, should have turned to Thornhill. (5) The chapel was built on the south side of the castle in the years 1721-3, and in the words of Maxwell Lyte, apparently under Thornhill's direction (6). It is the purpose of this article to test that assertion by a presentation of the evidence, both written and pictorial, which exercise also reveals something of Thornhill's methods as well as going far to establishing what the exterior and interior appearances of the chapel were like.

The chapel, alas, no longer exists, having been demolished when major alterations were made to the castle by Anthony Salvin between 1869 and 1872.(7). Only Thornhill's large painting of Moses and the Brazen Serpent, which once hung in the chapel, is still extant, it having been transferred to the Parish and Priory Church of St. George in Dunster where it yet remains for all to see (8). The written evidence on the chapel is to be found for the most part in the Luttrell family papers which were all deposited in the Somerset County record office in Taunton when Dunster Castle was given to the National Trust in 1976 (9).

Dorothy's new chapel at Dunster. South Front adjacent right hand tower. The classical niches still remain today in same place on the Library block. This is believed to be the very last photograph of the chapel before Anthony Salvin set to work on renovations in 1868.

The relevant documents are fourfold, the first of which is the estimate for the building. On the outside of this document is written:

An [illegible]
Of the Chappel
In Somersetshire

On the inside, in a beautiful copperplate hand (quite definitely not that of Thornhill) is written:

An Estimate of the Building of the Chappel
Supposing it were to be done in London where
Portland Stone is 2s a foote Cubical, Workmanship
Of Moldings 1s 6d a foot, and Plain Workmanship
1s 2d foot.
22 Rods of Brickwork at £5. 10s the Rod £121-0
1500 feet Supply of Ashlar Stone to case the outer
Wall at 2s. 0d the foot 150-0
340 feet Supply of Coin Stones at 3s the foot 51-0
The Stone Doorcase and Paving and Step 70-0
The Four Windows of Stone 100-0
The Plinth of the Building of Stone 20-0
The Cornice at the eaves and Pediment 300-0
The Round Window 3-0
Paving the Chappel with plain Stone 22-10
Paving and Steps at the Altar 25-0
Four Iron Windows and Casements with glass
and Painting in toto 54-0
Carpenters' Work of the Roof, Boarding for Lead,
Coving and Floors for
The Seats 86-0
Joiners Work of Seats and Outer Door 60-0
Joiners Work at the Altar 120-0

Plasterers Work 15-0
Plumbers Work in the Covering and Pipes 100-0
£1297-10

Although Thornhill's name is not specifically attached to the document, it is seems most likely in the light of subsequent correspondence that it came from his office, and its presumed origin in London where Thornhill worked, and there may be a hint too in the reference to Portland stone, the quarries for which were under the control of his close friend and political associate Edward Tucker, Surveyor of His Majesty's Quarries, Ways, Cranes and Piers in Portland and Mayor from time to time of Thornhill's parliamentary constituency, Weymouth and Melcombe Regis.

Under the second heading, there is a mass of accounts, being:

The Disbursements of William
Withycombe for my Honourable Mistress
Madam Dorothy Luttrell for the
Building ye Chaple in ye year 1722.

The accounts actually start in 1721 with payments for stone:

March 9th 1721 paid Robert Baker 4 days to draw stone at Pereton quarry (in the vicinity)

And this goes on until April 27th when Thomas Arney is paid 5s 11d for five and half days with board. The accounts start again in the next year when William Withycombe records:

June 9th 1722 Then the Chapple works began

There follows a list of payments for haulage, lime, stone labour, plumbing, plastering, timber and the sawing thereof. Payments go on right through 1723. These disbursements give interesting insight into the material used and the organisation, progress and accounting of a building project at this time, but there is no hint of the architect here.

Thirdly, and more importantly for the purpose of this article, there are three letters written by Francis Gwyn to Dorothy Luttrell concerning the internal decoration of the Chapel, which date from February and March 1723. Gwyn was a kinsman to Dorothy and he acted as intermediary between her and Thornhill in London. The letters are short and are best quoted in full:

Whitehall Feb 19 1722/3

Madam
Sir James Thornhill has now finished the draft for the Inside of your Chaple only desires to look it over once more for halfe an hour, to give such particular directions that your workmen may not mistake; I think it is very handsome, and he sayth it will

in his opinion come within the expence you proposed; you will have noe other tymber for wainscot (than) Deal which is to be painted of the stone colour (to answer) the Pilasters which are to be of the stucco; the Wainscot is to be about four foot and halfe high, as soon as Sir James hath perfected the Draft, I will send it downe to you and he will procure a Workman to come downe to you and finish the stucco worke and agree with him by the yard before he comes downe; I should be glad to have the opportunity to send downe the Draft in a Box that it may not be rumpled and wore out as the other was: which will make it plainer to be worked upon. I am Madam after this to return you my thanks for the 3 potts of laver, which is the best I ever tasted; I am Madam with great respect

Your most faithful Kinsman and obedient humble servant.
Francis Gwyn.

Whitehall March 2nd 1722/3

I had Madam the Honour of Your Letter of the 23rd of the last month, and had reason to hope that I should have sent the Draft to my Cousin Yarde this morning that it might have come to you in her Box, but Sir James Thornhill is at present gone to Greenwich (13), and will returne again on Monday. He had the Draft again from me finding it necessary to add some further directions that the workmen might not mistake in the Execution of it.

The Dutch oake will certainly doe very well for any of the wainscot; price the workmen say it is as cheap as Deal; I mentioned Deal s...it might be painted of the stone colour, as the Stucco Worke is: Therefore if Deal is cheaper it may doe as well: and then the Ditch oake may be made use of for the Benches and Pulpit.

I shall have the Draft (God willing) to send to downe by the carryer on Saturday next; and shall send it my Cousin Yarde in good time to convey it; I am Madam

With very true respect

Your most faithful Kinsman

And servant

Francis Gwyn

Whitehal March 9th 1722/3

I could not Madam answere your letter sooner which hath been soe long in my hands till I could acquaint you that this day I sent the draft perfected by Sir James Thornhill to my Cousin Yarde by her servant who called for it; so that it will come down to you in a box of hers by the carryer tomorrow.

I think it extreemly handsome, and Sir James assures me it will not be dear; I doe not doubt but that he described every thing soe well that your workmen will comprehend it, and you may begin as soon as you please upon the wainscot worke. The Draft which is made for the ceiling will be very handsome and is to be done by the same Playsterer; Sir James will find out such a Man fit for your Purse; contract with him by the yard and send him downe to you, so that I hope you will be at a certainty with him. The Festoons (as Sir James calls them) which are between the Pilasters and the Windows, are not to be don with stucco but Sir James will send down a man who shall

... them in paint without any great Charge when all the rest is don, and the work is ready for it what ever is wanting to Explain to the workmen may be pleased to let me know it, and you shall have further explanations; but I hope it is pretty plain, and will not need it.

I have a bad pen and ink, but could not omit giving you an Answer by this post and assuring you I am Madam with greatest respect

Your most faithful Kinsman
And humble servant
Francis Gwyn

It is reasonable to conclude from these letters that Thornhill was indeed the architect, and it must be beyond doubt that he was responsible for the interior decoration. The documents as a whole confirm too that the main body of the chapel was constructed in 1722 from June onwards, though work on the quarrying of the stone had begun in 1721, the remaining work, along with the interior decorations, being completed in all probability in November 1723.

The fourth document, the Will of Dorothy Luttrell (14), confirms that the work was finished after her death on 19th November 1723, for she specifies:

I give and bequeath
Unto Sir John Trevelyan Baronet and the said Mr Kymer (15) the summe of Three Hundred and fifty pounds to be laid out in

*the finishing and compleating the Chappel which I have
already begun.*

Payments were indeed made thereafter. There is one on
24th November 1723 for five loads of stone from
Minehead Bay for the Chapel (£0.10.0), another for two
hogsheads of lime on the 29th, and on the 12th December
we have paid to Thomas Partridge for 12 days Work
helping Mr Sidnall (?) about the Chapel 0.12.0. On the
16th December old Mr Withycombe and his son are paid
£146.05.3½, also for work on the Chapel. The work seems
then to have been complete.

If these documents then serve to confirm Thornhill's
standing as architect as well as a painter, they also serve
to show us something of the man and his business
methods. He is at pains to make sure that the work does
not cost more than the estimate and acts as agent in
contracting out work to artisans whose ability he knew and
at a rate carefully fixed beforehand. Nowadays, one would
expect the architect to have a hand in the supervision of
the building work; in those days, given the great difficulties
of travel, especially in the winter, this cannot have been a
practical proposition when the work was to be done, as
with this chapel, far afield. Hence the need to act through
a kinsman of the client and the great care that Thornhill
takes in making absolutely sure that the Draft will be
readily comprehensible to the workmen on the spot. This
must, of course, have been easier when the workmen were
chosen by and known to him. The one regret is that the

Draft referred to and, indeed, all the other plans, are lost. Perhaps when the work was done they too were so rumpled and wore out as not to be thought worth preserving.

Dorothy Luttrell's new chapel in centre, south front, with gleaming white Portland stone façade. The Madam Luttrell mentioned above in the advert is Dorothy Luttrell. Trees on the Dunster Estate were prized by shipwrights as being ideal for Great Britain's navy.

Dorothy Luttrell's chapel demolished to make way for huge Drawing Room tower on south side

CHAPTER 9

MARGARET FOWNES LUTTRELL, THE CHILD HEIRESS

Margaret Fownes Luttrell, 1726-1766

Heiress with ten children

Margaret Luttrell, the only child of Alexander Luttrell, well deserves mention in my list of illustrious ladies, having borne ten children of her own and being just eleven years old when she inherited a debt-ridden Dunster Castle. Also at this time there were only five living relatives of Luttrells in England. Two young girls, this Margaret and her cousin Anne; Southcote Luttrell, described as a lunatic from Saunton Court, Devon; an old bachelor called Francis Luttrell of the Temple; and a boy called Southcote Hungerford Luttrell, who was the father of Edward Luttrell, surgeon, and went on to found the Australian branch. These last three were distantly related to the Luttrells of Dunster, with no ancestor in residence for two centuries.

Margaret Fownes Luttrell by Richard Phelps, Porlock

Alexander Luttrell had died in debt, due in part to his personal extravagance and in part to the necessity imposed upon him by his parents of providing a fortune of £10,000 for Anne Luttrell mentioned above and daughter of his deceased brother Francis. The estate was again thrown into Chancery and it wasn't until 1744 that the Master entrusted with the estate made his report upon the accounts.

In the meantime Dunster Castle was closed and two valuations of its contents were made for the satisfaction of the creditors, though all the paintings and furniture were saved, but such silver as had been acquired by Alexander Luttrell was dispersed. The accounts of Lancelot St Albyn, the receiver of the rents for the year 1743, contain several references to this matter, including:

"Paid Mr Alexander, goldsmith, for his assistance of three days at the sale of Mr Luttrell's plate, £2. 4s 6d. Paid Mr White for the use of a room in the Crown Tavern in Taunton, three days and expenses there, £2. 1s 5d. Paid the cryer, or salesman, 5s."

Details have been preserved of the weight of every piece sold, and it is interesting to note that they range from 4s 8d to 6s 6d per ounce. The names of the purchasers are also given and among them were Sir John Trevelyan, Margaret Luttrell's grandfather, George Trevelyan, her uncle and Mrs Dyke, her mother, all of whom have family portraits in Dunster Castle. There were also St Albyn, her agent, and Alexander, the goldsmith at Taunton. The yearly value of Margaret Luttrell's estate at this period was about £6,300, though the actual rental was only £2,150 because most of the farms and other buildings were let on lease for the lives of the tenants.

Margaret Luttrell spent many years under the roof of her stepfather, Edward Dyke, a very moderate sum being allowed for her maintenance and education, which included music lessons. It was from this house at Tetton, Kingston St Mary near Taunton, that she was married to her second cousin, Henry Fownes of Nethway, Brixham, Devon. The ceremony took place at Kingston Court on 16th February 1747, when she was just twenty-one years of age, and so free from the control of guardians, lawyers and the like. The union proved very happy and her letters to her husband, written when she was parted from him, are conceived with sincere affection. At times she acted as his secretary. Her health, however was not good, and she died on the 13th August 1766, having given birth to ten children. She was buried among the vaults with her ancestors at St George's Church, Dunster.

There are four portraits of Margaret at the castle. In the first one in the Drawing Room she is represented as a small child in white muslin with bare feet offering cherries to a bird in the middle of a large canvas. Afterwards she was painted by a Porlock artist called Richard Phelps who was in residence at the time. He it was who designed Conigar Tower, the two bridges with their rapids and waterfall over the River Avill and the 'gothic' archway next to the watermill in the gardens. In this portrait Margaret is depicted three-quarter length in her grey and blue satin with a string of pearls around her neck which can be seen on the Grand Staircase mezzanine at the castle. A third painting shows her in a grey cloak trimmed with lace, and lace around her head. The fourth painting gives only the head and neck with an open lace collar. There is a fifth painting of Margaret Luttrell at Bathealton Court, near Taunton, painted some time after her marriage.

Margaret's ten children were Alexander, born on March 1749, died June the same year, John, Henry, Alexander, Francis, Thomas, who became Lieutenant-Colonel in the Somerset Fencible Infantry, Margaret (Peggy), who was later painted by Sir Joshua Reynolds – her portrait is now in the Dining Room – Anne, Anne and a third Anne, all three of whom died within months of being born.

On her death in 1766 Margaret Fownes Luttrell, the heiress of Dunster Castle and estates, left her husband a widower for several years. However, he married in 1771 Frances, daughter of Samuel Bradley of Dunster, who had claimed descent from the Luttrells through Frances' mother. After Henry Fownes Luttrell's death in 1780 she resided in Taunton but was buried at Dunster church in 1803.

Below is a survey of Margaret Luttrells estates in 1746

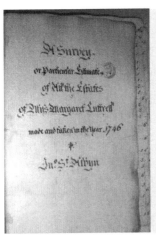

On 16 February 1747, when she came of age, in Kingston St Mary Church she married her second cousin Henry Fownes (d.1780) of Nethway House, Kingswear (historically in Brixham), Devon. Both shared as a great-grandfather Edward Yard (1638–1703) of Churston Ferrers, MP for Ashburton in 1685, who himself was a grandson of Thomas Fownes (d.1635), Mayor of Plymouth in 1619. On their marriage Dunster Castle became the property of her husband (married women in England were not allowed to own property until 1882), who adopted the additional surname Luttrell after his own, and adopted the Luttrell arms (but continued to quarter Fownes), in accordance with a stipulation in Alexander Luttrell's will. They moved into Dunster Castle and updated the interior with Chinese painted wallpaper and new furniture in a Rococo style. New windows were installed in the stair hall and dining room. The marriage was a happy one and resulted in the birth of ten children, including:

- John Fownes Luttrell (1752–1816), eldest son and heir, of Dunster Castle, MP for Minehead (1776–1816), the Luttrell pocket borough adjacent to Dunster Castle;[11]

- Lieutenant Henry Fownes-Luttrell (1753–1777), 2nd son, who died unmarried.[11]

- Rev. Alexander Fownes Luttrell (born 1754), 3rd son, Rector of East Quantoxhead, which manor had been held by the Luttrells since 1232, and Vicar of Minehead.[11][12]

- Francis Fownes Luttrell (1756–1823), 4th son, a barrister of the Middle Temple, a commissioner of customs and MP for Minehead 1780-3;[11]

- Lt-Col. Thomas Fownes Luttrell (1763–1811), 5th son

- Margaret Fownes-Luttrell (1747-1792), only daughter, whose three portraits are on display in Dunster Castle, one as an adult by Sir Joshua Reynolds (with a copy) and another as an infant by Phelps. She married John Henry Southcote (1747) on 24 May 1769. They had two daughters.

After her death John married Priscilla Aston and they had three sons and a daughter. They were Josias Southcote (1798), Henry Aston (born Southcote) (1804-1888) (Note: he was baptised again in 1821 as Henry Aston), Isabella Southcote (1809) and Thomas Southcote (1812).

Margaret Fownes-Luttrell died on 13 August 1766 and was buried at Dunster Castle.

Two of her works are located at the castle, in the National Trust collection:

Margaret Fownes-Luttrell, View of an Imaginary Castle with a Round Tower

Margaret Fownes-Luttrell, View of an Imaginary Castle with Two Towers. Watercolour on paper, Dunster Castle and Dunster Church, Somerset by Margaret Fownes-Luttrell, Mrs John Henry Southcote (1747-1792). Label on back 'Dunster Castle painted by Mrs Luttrell and presented to Mrs W. George January 16th 1900.

Margaret Luttrell (1726–1766), by Richard Phelps, Porlock.

CHAPTER 10

AMELIA ANNE HOOD, A DISTINGUISHED VICTORIAN LADY

1790-1883

I had originally omitted Amelia from our list of the women of Dunster simply because she did not carry the name Luttrell, but on second thoughts I reinstated her, as her daughter, Anne Elizabeth Periam Hood, married George Fownes Luttrell and also because she often resided at Dunster Castle and helped pay the costs of Dunster Church's major Victorian rebuilding, though she was not a parishioner.

Amelia Anne was born in Tidlake, Surrey in 1790, the daughter of Sir Hugh Bateman of Harrington Hall, Derby, who married in 1829 Isobel Harriet, daughter of Sir Peregrine Palmer-Fuller-Palmer-Ackland whose name he

assumed. Her husband was Sir Alexander Hood MP of
Wooton Butleigh near Glastonbury, whose father, Captain

Amelia Anne Hood by John Lucas, 59 x 47. Oil on canvas.

Alexander Hood, married one Elizabeth Periam. George Fownes Luttrell was eventually to marry, in 1852, Amelia Anne's daughter, a certain Anne Elizabeth Periam Hood*, sister of Arthur, Lord Hood of Avalon.

I first met Amelia when entering our Library. A distinguished person indeed. Her portrait by John Lucas reveal her standing with her right hand resting on a classical urn containing geraniums surrounded by ivy under the shade of a beech tree, where in the background on Windmill Hill, Somerset, can be seen the naval memorial or Butleigh monument dedicated to the seafaring Hood family. Amelia's hair is smoothly parted in the middle and drawn tight across her head into a bun at the back, which allowed side clusters to frame the face. A lace frill and ribbon bows adorn her hair and her shawl is black square cashmere of soft goat's wool. Her brooch is attached to a choker and crepe de chine is embroidered in silk and heavily fringed. Her daughter, Elizabeth Periam Hood, is in another portrait on an adjacent wall and above the fireplace in Library.

*On August 17th 1901 this Elizabeth, her husband George Luttrell and their daughter were involved in an accident when their carriage collided with a lorry at Williton. The carriage was badly damaged, one of the horses was severely cut and the other knocked to the ground. None of the occupants were hurt.

St George's Church before renovation. Etching by Elizabeth Piper,
Clifton School of Art, Bristol

One year after the completion of the restoration and
renovation of Dunster Castle in 1874, a complete
restoration of St George's Church was announced. The

architect was Mr G Street, who was supported by George Luttrell and his wife Elizabeth. The work was done by local men regularly employed on the manor under the able supervision of Mr Samson, the churchwarden.

Amelia Anne Hood, George's mother in law, generously paid £3,000 to aid repairs and restoration. She knew the extent of the work about to be undertaken in 1875 as a well-known architect called J. C. Buckler had visited the Luttrells in 1838 and painted a delightful watercolour of James Thornhill's chapel on the South Front. This watercolour is reproduced in various guidebooks of the castle.

Following centuries of decline in the woollen industry and the disappearance of wealth at Dunster, Buckler found that St George's Church was in dire need of urgent repairs and stated, 'With regard to the eastern part, or 'old church'... the walls were shattered and infirm in places, that the roof was very defective and covered with a thick coat of moss... that the mullions and tracery of the windows were dilapidated and ruinous and that the floors were stripped of its pavements and strewn with canopied monuments and various kinds of rubbish.'

Buckler's language had an immediate effect, and many of his recommendations were followed. In the middle of the eighteenth century the church was in a dilapidated state, with parts of it used as a depository for all kinds of rubbish. The windows were broken and rotted and the pavements were uneven, cracked and broken. The Chapel of St Lawrence was a mere ruin barely protected by a rough slanting roof, whilst stone walls shut the church off from the north and south transepts, the north part being the priory or Luttrell chapel. This was the part used by the Benedictine monks until the Dissolution of the Monasteries. Apparently the vicar of the time had the beautiful rood screen painted white.

The sanitary facilities too were in a terrible state. Families who held pews in the church, including the Luttrells, were accustomed to burying their dead beneath the floors of their pews in shallow brick graves. These graves when opened were frequently found to be filled with black foetid water, in which the coffins floated or had turned over, or in some cases had split open to reveal rotten flesh, bones and clothes. This state of affairs would have shocked a Victorian lady such as Amelia Ann. The church windows were also in a terrible state.

A complete restoration was begun under the sensitive guidance of the architect G. E. Street, ably assisted by G. H. Samson, who saw the work through to completion. These days the restoration might be done differently, but as Dr Francis Eeles wrote: "Very great care was taken in every detail and Mr Street's new fittings are marked by dignity and restraint." A large Perpendicular window at the east end of the church was removed and replaced by three thirteenth century style Lancet windows constructed from remains found in the vicinity of the church by Mr Samson.

Other Victorian glass in the church postdates the restoration. The next window west of the window 'of an earlier date' in the south choir was erected in 1882 to the memory of yet another Luttrell lady, Emma Louisa Fownes Luttrell (1798-1881), widow of Francis Fownes Luttrell, and her daughter Augusta Margaret Luttrell (1825-1880). This window had recently been inserted on the south side of the choir and was manufactured by Clayton and Bell. It was insured for £100 in 1891.

The west doorway was enlarged and new choir stalls, enclosed by screens, were put up in what was to be known as the Priory Church. The gallery and box pews were removed and a new high altar was set up under the central tower. Part of the screen that now crossed between the eastern arches of the tower was moved to the curiously shaped thirteenth century arch in the south transept, which had been previously widened in the fifteenth or sixteenth centuries.

The last window before the 1499 screen is of 'cathedral' glass. Going clockwise round the church, to the east of the south porch door the next window was erected after the death of Amelia Anne, widow of Sir Alexander Hood, at the castle in 1883. It was another lady, Elizabeth Periam Fownes Luttrell, her daughter, who dedicated the window to her, and to these ladies must be given the credit of placing the plans for the great restoration of the church in the hands of Mr G. Street. Credit for the construction of the castle goes to Elizabeth Periam and her husband George Luttrell for giving Anthony Salvin the plans. There is a window in the church dedicated to her memory with the tracery lights bearing scrolls with the inscription, "He shall give his angels charge over thee". The subject of the three main lights is our Lord blessing little children and beneath are the words, "He took them up in His arms, put His hands upon them, and blessed them." At the bottom of the window is the inscription, "To the Glory of God and in loving memory of Amelia Anne Hood widow of Sir Ackland Hood of Wooton died at Dunster Castle 31st January, 1883, aged 84, dedicated by her daughter, Ann Fownes Luttrell"

It is strange that St George's Church holds no memory to Amelia's husband except that the whole restoration was a tribute to his generosity, and the existing Victorian work is a constant reminder. It is also one of the very few English churches to have a carillon, installed during renovations in 1886, a system where tunes are played on the church bells every four hours, with a different tune for each day of the week.

The cost of the restoration was in excess of £12,000, of which George Luttrell contributed almost £10,000, Lady Amelia £3,000 and other repair costs from the Rev Todd and several people connected with Dunster Castle. Three months after the opening of the church in 1876 the vicar noted a further gift by Lady Hood, 'two handsome standards of thirteen lights, each the work of Mess. Potters of South Molton".

The Luttrell burial ground extends on three sides of the Priory Church. Prior to the Reformation it had been a part of the Priory gardens, but was in the possession of the Luttrells after the Dissolution of the Monasteries,

St George's Church, after renovation in 1876

when Dame Margaret Wyndham bought the Priory around 1540.

Elizabeth Periam Hood's family were from the seafaring naval family called the 'Hood Brothers' by Admiral Horatio Nelson. The British battleship of the same name was sunk by the German battleship Bismarck at the Battle of the Denmark Strait in 1941.

CHAPTER 11

ALYS ANN LUTTRELL

1888-1974

Creative gardener and supporter of the community

Dunster must be one of the few communities in the country that is still a vibrant working village situated within a Grade I historic landscape, and part of this area was Alys Luttrell's domain. Australian-born Alys enjoyed immense fame at Dunster Castle during her own time, and is one of my favourite châtelaines. We owe her for all the gardens around the Tor. The terraces and slopes round the castle have developed from military defences to formal gardens in the eighteenth century and to the shady wild walks we enjoy today. The mild sea air ensures balmy winters so that on the slopes of the tor tropical and sub-tropical plants flourish, and the palm trees, mimosa and lemon and banana bring an exotic sparkle to the walk downhill to from the house to the river Avill which flows from Dunkery Beacon through the south flank of the tor.

On its banks stand the great Castle Mill with picturesque classical bridges and rustic gothic gateway. The mill at present derives mainly from the eighteenth century, but it replaced earlier medieval mills along the south tor which can be traced back to the Domesday Book of 1086. Thanks to Alys' love of her native Australia this whole garden area remains a delight of species brought from her homeland, and indeed from the Himalayas and South America.

In the 1920s and 30s at least seven gardeners were employed by Alys in the castle grounds and the complex of walled gardens under a head gardener. The gardens and shrubberies were recalled by R. J. Pearse, who had worked in the gardens in 1933, as well maintained and home to rare shrubs and trees such as banana trees, tree ferns and tropical bamboos planted in the Mill Walks and all around the castle.

The gardens included a melon garden and two gardens in Mill Lane where there were two vegetable gardens growing asparagus, celery, marrows and also various fruit trees including apple – Bramleys, Allison's Orange, Cox's Orange Pippin and Lord Lambourne, as well as quinces. June Copp, long-serving room volunteer, tells us that young lads were employed by Alys to carry baskets of fruit and vegetables up to her in the castle. During the Second World War, Land Army Girls Margaret Parham, Ann Dunn and Alice Down were employed to work in the castle gardens and nursery.

A quote from Somerset Life Magazine in 1990 by John Sales tells us: "The site with its extraordinary variety of aspect, exposure and soil conditions creates unmatched opportunities for the plantsman, inspiration for the designer and a challenge for the gardener, and is a setting for an astonishing diversity."

Below a letter from Treseder Nurseries to Alys in 1964

Nurseries mentioned by Alys Luttrells' in Garden Book:

- Cowpit Road Nurseries (Dept1) Spalding
- Burkwood and Skipworth, Ltd Park Rd Nurseries, Kingston on Thames Surrey
- Elm Garden Nurseries Chrurch Rd Claygate
- Samuel Dobie and Son Ltd 11, Grovenor St??
- Hillier and Sons Winchester
- Haskin Bros Coy Pond Nurseries Bournemouth West
- Outwell Bulb Co. (1959) Ltd (dept. EB) Outwell Nr Wisbech, Cambs
- Nyssen (Bulbs) Lyd Railway Rd Urmston Manchester
- S I Newbury 273 Dallow Rd Luton Beds
- Gerago Telkamp Hillegom Holland (Bramber, Steyning Sussex)
- John Scott &Co The Royal Nurseries Merriot
- Wallace and Barr The Old Gardens Bayham Rd Tunbridge Wells
- ?? 26, Clarendon Park Clacton on Sea Essex

TRESEDERS' NURSERIES (TRURO) LTD

(I. G. TRESEDER, N. G. TRESEDER, M. L. TRESEDER)

Landscape Gardeners, Nurserymen and Seedsmen

NURSERY STOCK
TWELVE ACRES

TELEPHONE 4371-2

NGT/OMS/1245

THE NURSERIES
TRURO, CORNWALL

11th May, 1964
Dictated on 9th May, 1964

Mrs. A. Luttrell,
Dunster Castle,
DUNSTER,
Somerset.

Dear Madam,

We acknowledge your letter and regret to hear that the plant of Dendromecon rigidum arrived in poor condition.

As this plant is very impatient of any root disturbance we doubt if it will recover and will make a note to send you a replacement plant in the autumn should it fail to do so, so will you kindly keep us acquainted with its conditions

We are passing on your comments to our dispatch department.

Yours faithfully,

TRESEDERS' NURSERIES (Truro) LTD.

6.10.64

This was all started by Dorothy Luttrell and continued with Anne Elizabeth Luttrell, Alice Edwina Luttrell and of course Alys Luttrell.

Alys met Geoffrey, her future husband, when he was Principle Private Secretary to the Governor General of Australia. He was invited to dine with Alys' father, Admiral Bridges, an Anglo-Scot living in Victoria, and that was how they met. Alys was born on 3rd March 1888 in Melbourne East, Victoria, Australia and married Geoffrey Luttrell in 1918. They had two sons, Geoffrey Walter, born in 1919, and Julian, born in 1932. In the late 1930s they adopted a daughter, Penelope, who was to marry into the Gaskell family. There is a photograph of Alys in the Drawing Room and several other showrooms of the castle.

Besides being honorary Vice President of the Somerset branch of the British Red Cross, Alys was closely connected with the Minehead and West Somerset Hospital, which had been founded in 1920 by her father-in-law Alexander. She served on several of the hospital committees, including the Linen League, whose function was to provide the hospital with extras. She was President of the Minehead and District TB care committee, which provided money and milk for local tuberculosis suffers.

She was president of the Dunster Nursing Association and invited its members to hold their annual meetings at the castle, where she entertained them to tea. She was also President of the Minehead District Nursing Association.

During World War II Alys was involved in many and varied causes for the general war effort. For instance she inaugurated West Somerset's Bomber and Fighter plane collections, and was President of the committee for Minehead District of the Penny-a-Week and Rural

Pennies Fund of the Red Cross, which raised over £7,500 from 1939 to 1945. After the war she was Vice President of the Somerset Marriage Guidance Council and President of the Bridgwater and Minehead Moral Welfare Association. In politics she was, like her husband, a Conservative and served on the Dunster and Minehead branches of the party.

Alys entertaining in the Drawing Room, Dunster Castle. NT Cartoon, Peter Stevenson

After World War II Alys became a member of the Management Committee of Broadlands Retirement Home, Minehead, giving the residents a TV set in 1953 so that they could watch the Coronation of Elizabeth II. From 1943 to 1944 she made the castle available for use as a convalescent home for naval and American military officers. She ran it like a big house party and for some time the castle was full up with 12 officers and staff, the faces continually changing as men recovered and others were admitted. She was also a member of the Exmoor Forces Welfare Committee.

After Geoffrey's death in 1957, Alys became the President of the West Somerset Archaeological Society. After the war archery was being developed at Dunster (reviving the example of Margaret Luttrell in 1431, who held competitions in Hanger Park or the Jousting Lawns) and claimed Alys' interest and support. Tourneys were held on the castle lawns and Alys was appointed President of the West Somerset Company of Archers and Lady Paramount of the South Western Archery Association, whose tournaments are still regularly held on the castle lawns or park.

Alys had close connections with the Dunster Mothers' Union, the women's section of the Dunster British Legion and the Minehead British Sailors' Society, which she founded. She was also one of the very few honorary life members of the National Council of Women, and she worked for various societies for the blind and the deaf.

She also had an interest in local people who were down on their luck. One such was a man called Timothy Bourne Whitby, who lived in a shack near Dunster Beach for almost twenty years. He was a man of education who took to vagrancy on the death of his wife. In the 1930s at Dunster and was held in affection by all who knew him, especially by holidaymakers on Dunster Beach. He enjoyed visits to the castle, where he discussed many matters with Alys Luttrell, who kept a caring eye on him.

In the 1950s the new owner of Dunster Beach had plans for expansion and offered Tim £50 to relocate. As he aged and became frail, Alys Luttrell offered him the opportunity to put his shack closer to the castle, and he lived there until his death. He is buried at Dunster and remembered as a remarkable man.

Alys loved flowers and took pride in the gardens, often called the finest in the south west. In her later years one of her favourite pastimes was to drive herself around the castle in her little electric chair, which she called her 'chariot', with her two dogs, often accompanied by the head gardener, to whom she would outline her plans for the various parts of the garden. She was President of the Dunster Horticultural Society and of the Minehead and District Choral Society and organised concerts at the castle.

Alys was strong-willed and could be autocratic at times, but she was also extremely kind and generous and she never put on airs. Before she became frail, she did a great deal of entertaining – balls, dinner parties, shooting parties and weekend visits. The most formal and elaborate functions were the balls, usually in aid of some charity.

She was also devoted to animals and had a deep concern for their welfare. She was a great dog lover, usually having two of her own. She was also an accomplished rider, and although in this country she always rode side saddle, in Australia she had often ridden astride. However she had a number of falls, which left her with a painful back problem.

She was an extremely good whip and right up to four years before her death was often to be seen driving her immaculately turned-out dog cart, pulled by a skewbald pony called Jigsaw, through the Minehead traffic. One of her ponies, named Jigsaw, died in 1963 at the age of 29 and is buried on the edge of the park just below the path to Lawns Bridge, where a memorial stands.

Alys did not always rely on a horse; at one time she owned one of the first Armstrong Siddeley cars to have an automatic gearbox.

Photograph of Alys and her Highland Terrier at Dunster Castle

Despite her busy life she still found time to write articles on her life at Dunster Castle (for Country Life Magazine) in which she described, amongst other things, the inadequacies of the heating and the plumbing, while pointing out that the castle had the first bathroom in Somerset. She also wrote the foreword to the Dunster Tourist Guide and was amazed by the new kitchen above the old Victorian one, put in whilst she was visiting her family in Australia.

Alys' son Julian said that, about two years after his father died in 1957, his mother decided she did not want a kitchen the size of the one downstairs (the Victorian kitchen). Julian was away "soldiering" at the time and he pointed out that there had been enormous changes after the war – financially, socially and in every possible direction – so a large kitchen was not required. "I think she wanted something nearer to the dining room, but I never heard it referred to as the Blue Kitchen – it was always The Pantry," he said. David (the House Manager) asked if his mother had any involvement in the kitchen and Julian confirmed that his brother, who had just come back from the war, probably did the basic organisation of the design, with his mother's approval (there is some discrepancy here, as Walter Luttrell had always said that his mother did not know that the Blue Kitchen was being installed). Julian said she never liked it, even though it was her idea to have it there. Walter confirmed that she did not like the Blue Kitchen – apparently after 45 years she missed going down the stairs, sitting at the table with the Chef and discussing the meals –but she accepted it.

The guests came from all over the county and beyond, and Mrs Luttrell used to stand in the Inner Hall to receive each couple as they entered. "She had a great many beautiful evening gowns and a large collection of jewellery," said Julian. "Being so tall and stately she looked wonderful in evening dress and was in her element as a charming hostess."

Alys's dream garden restored at Dunster Castle

However these social events took their toll, and Alys sometimes became so exhausted that she had to spend a day or two in bed to recuperate. She also suffered from rheumatism, which gradually became worse and made climbing the stairs difficult. In her later years she used the morning room as her main living room as it gave her level access to her bedroom. Towards the end of her life her memory deteriorated and she became vague and forgetful. "Sadly she lost much of her indomitable spirit and later became bedridden," said Julian. Finally she went into a coma and passed peacefully away on November 12 1974 at the age of 86. Her funeral service was held on the Saturday. In its obituary the West Somerset Free Press called Alys "The gracious Chatelaine of Dunster Castle, friend and supporter of good causes and a figure whose leadership and influence in valuable works undertaken in county and district for the public good will long be remembered. Hundreds of people came to know her, as she moved about in her many spheres of interest in her active years as a personality of great charm and friendliness."

Alys wrote the following letter to Miss Val Piper-Smith (Val, a long serving Room Volunteer at the castle, had written to Alys wishing her a speedy recovery):

"I am happy when people feel the, to me, lovely atmosphere of my home which seems to have stood for courage and steadfastness and peaceful serenity (despite its warring history) all these many centuries. What a charming gift you sent me – nothing could have given me greater delight, especially as I had to "stay put" in my room with laryngitis and the sight of the lovely flowers meant a lot to me."

Mrs J. Mill, who had been a secretary in the Foreign Office during World War II, wrote: "I did for some months deal with Mrs Luttrell's personal letters, and came to know the family quite well. In fact I used to join them for breakfast, and my husband used to breakfast in the American Air Force Mess. That generation of the family must have all died and I have lost touch, being myself in my 80s. Mrs Luttrell was charming and very friendly. "

A personal account from Alys:

As romantic as any Rhineland eyrie
My home, Dunster Castle, dates from the eleventh century, when it was granted by William the Conqueror to William de Mohun, and was considered to be the strongest fortress in the West Country.

Admiral Blake, under the orders of Cromwell, besieged it for 160 days but failed to take it, and though in the end he subdued the garrison by starvation, he allowed them to march out with honours of war. The keep and many of the defences were, however, demolished.

After that the castle became more of a dwelling house, but still retained its unique position on the summit of a tor overlooking the picturesque village and the Bristol Channel. Rising a hundred feet above the castle is the keep, and, nearby, an oubliette filled with bones of unfortunates who tried to scale the sheer sides of the tor.

My husband's family have lived here since 1936, and from time to time the castle has been altered and modernized. The upper dungeons, for instance, have been turned into kitchens and larders, although the old dungeons are still dark and dank below. When the kitchen was altered in the last century it was doubtless the last word in modernization, with an enormous heated table in the centre and an immense dresser loaded with gleaming copper pots and pans.

A big mechanical spit was operated from the huge range. Nowadays, however, I look with envy on the colourful and convenient kitchens of my friends, with no forty-yard trek to the larders.

Heating is our biggest problem, and plumbing a close second – although we had the first bathroom in Somerset. The greatest change since I came here in 1920 has been the opening of the castle to the public. As it has no state rooms, there is little privacy for us and, on open days, lunch must be eaten at great speed before the family retires to the library – one of the few rooms not on view.

Though the indoor staff is greatly reduced from the good old days, we manage – with the aid of vacuum cleaners, polishers and now a dish-washing machine – to keep the house in reasonable order.

The Great Hall fills a large part of the ground floor – with the Banqueting Hall, hung with painted leather panels, above – and many little staircases lead to rooms on different levels.

There are beautiful views from every window – looking north across the channel to Wales, and south up the fertile valley of the Avill to the heather-clad slopes of Dunkery Beacon.

The gardens are in bits and on various levels. There is a small formal terrace where in sun and shelter, palms grow and Banksia roses, clematis and semi-tropical plants cling to the old grey-pink walls. Camellias flourish against a fifty-foot yew hedge and, down by the stream, bananas, bamboos and ferns are happy among rhododendrons and gay azaleas.

Are there ghosts at Dunster? I don't see them. To me it is a stately, gentle, happy castle.

Sir Walter Luttrell's account of Alys:

My mother was a beautiful rider. She rode almost entirely sidesaddle. She used to ride astride in Australia, but she always hunted sidesaddle and went like a rocket. But she'd had a lot of cracking falls in Australia, riding these virtually unbroken horses out there and she had a very bad back and it used to play her up.

So, very often she'd say – because nobody ever had a horsebox in those days, and we used to go on and meet up at Raleigh's Cross which was an hour, pretty well two hours' ride on – and she used to say, would I take her horse on? Well, that was all right, I did, I often rode that on. What one did then was take the pommel out, and just sling a leg loose the other side, and you only just walked or jogged.

But there was one occasion when I was out on my feet, with the Minehead Harriers, and she was riding and her back suddenly gave way. So, I was at a gate actually, I'd opened it for them, and she said, you know, "I can't go on. Would you like to take the horse on?" This was a horse called Peacock, which I knew very well, and I'd ridden lots of times. So I said, "All right," and I climbed up sidesaddle. And I must say, I'd ridden a lot but I'd never been so frightened in my life, because if you look down on this side, the right hand side, it's just like sitting on the edge of Beachy Head, you know, because there's absolutely nothing between you and Mother Earth. Anyway we went on and had great fun, we had a very good hunt, so at least I can claim I've once ridden to hounds sidesaddle.

Alys Luttrell, second from left, with the Maharaja of Jaipur on the steps of Dunster Castle Entrance Porch.

Alys had kept a diary for over forty years but just before her death she wrote a note saying all the volumes should now be burnt. This was a tragedy, as another fascinating insight into life and times of Dunster Castle could have been gleaned. Julian Luttrell wrote:

Mother was an outstanding gardener, not only in terms of design, and she was not in any way a qualified garden designer, but she had her own splendid ideas in terms of what she would like to see.

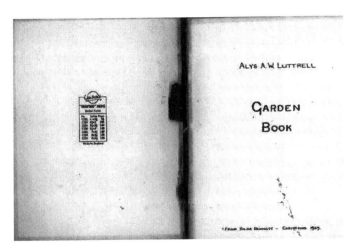

Alys Luttrell's Garden Book

This book is really rather fascinating because in here are all the plants that were grown in various parts of the garden, giving you the names of the nurseries they came from and the dates when they were received, what the price was and the whole lot. A lot of these no longer exist. Here you are, for example, begonias, macrophyllia, centaura, right the way through. These are all the plants that she wished to plant here. Obviously some have gone, some removed but it is a record in my lifetime of the enormous amount of effort she put into choosing plants, and you have the record of where they came from.

In here you will see Antony Estate Nurseries – that does not exist any more, but my mother used to go down and visit them. It was the most lovely nursery. Of course in those days garden centres did not exist and you were either a nurseryman or a plantsman. This is 1959/60 – Inglewood nurseries, which still exist. Timsbury nurseries, types of azaleas. Robert Beech, they are still going. We have masses of letters of apology from various gardeners if a plant was not a very good specimen, or after my mother wrote a letter praising them. This is her garden book for the most active time that she was here gardening. It is a wonderful record of the 1960s when the garden was "done up" after the war. You can see the type of plants she had.

The Dream Garden

Julian Luttrell confirmed that the Dream Garden was always called that. Robin Andrews, Head Gardener, explains that the plan is to restore the Dream Garden to the way it was.

Julian says it was all done with box hedging.

It was kept mainly as a private garden, although people going to church were allowed to walk through the gate which is next door to what we call Snapes Cottage. On the left was where Mr Hargreaves and Mr Heritage, the Head Gardeners, lived, in the cottage just as you go into West Street on the left hand side. I think the garden was laid out in about 1930. It was done over a period of time. If you are walking into the Dream Garden from the West Street entrance, then the area on the left was the last bit to be done. The rectangle was done first and then it was laid out first of all by a firm called Tresidder, who don't exist any more. They were great landscape gardeners from Cornwall. They laid out the basic plan, my mother chose the planting and along the wall there were all climbers, which were rather lovely. There were three seats, one at either end and one in the old bit.

PART 2
Women in trouble

Wife beating husband with distaff. c. 14th century
Illustration from The Luttrell Psalter. British Library, London

INTRODUCTION

Colourful as the stories of the châtelaines of Dunster are, they are mild compared to some of the adventures of other women associated with the castle. There were family feuds settled (or not) with axes and arrows, pikes and bills; a pickpocket who was chained to a wheelbarrow; a female commander directing murderous cannon fire; a woman burned to death; and a husband thrown out of a top window at Court House. There are tales of greed, missing gold and silver, of adulteresses, illegal marriages, excommunication, a stillborn child and graveyard gold. Here are some highlights.

CHAPTER 1

A FAMILY FEUD

Sir Andrew Luttrell was the father of Sir John Luttrell. When there was a major disagreement between the servants of Sir Andrew Luttrell and his mother-in-law, Dame Walthean Yard, over inheritance, the servants decide to settle the matter, and old scores, on the Quantock hills whilst Andrew and Walthean were locked in legal proceedings in London in 1521.

Sir Andrew Luttrell, who had been attendant upon Anne Boleyn at her coronation ceremony in 1533, had quarrelled many times with his stepmother, Dame Walthean, for she kept him out of much of his inheritance. In reply to a bill filed against her in the Star Chamber, she stated that her stepson Andrew Luttrell had: "in Lent last past, because of his wilfull and cruel mind, without any reasonable cause, took her goods and chatells, not leaving her dish, pot, nor pan, and that she and her children and servants had stood in daily peril of their lives," until she went up to London, leaving only a certain Lewis Griffyth and an "impotent, power" almsman, eighty years of age, to look after her interests at East Quantoxhead. One of Andrew Luttrell's servants, John Gay by name, complained to the King's Council in counter suit that, on the 7th of June, 1521: "Lewis Griffyth and several other evil-disposed persons assaulted him at East Quantoxhead, shot eleven arrows at him, one of which pierced him through the left arm, while others greviously struck him in different places of his bod, so that and if succour of trees had not been close at hand, they would have killed and murdered him out of hand." He also said that he had received "a great wound in the shoulder" from a forest bill.

Lewis Griffyth's account of the matter is much more detailed, he having been there in Quantock Park. He recalled:

With his bow and his shafts under his girdle, going about to recover a deer, being hurt, in a place called Blakwell, met the said John Gay and two other men. Gay was armed with a peaked staff seven feet long, and his companions carried great axes. They said that they had come, by command of their master (Andrew Luttrell) to take sixty trees for posts, but he told them that this could not be done without warrant from Dame Walthean, who held the manor for her life.

Furthermore, he "to fear the said John Gay and his

fellows, shot an arrow wide of them." When Gay asked him "to holde his hand," he "took his cap in his hand and desyered and tenderly prayed them to departe". This they did, but they "wente into a place withyn the said towne and there harrassed them, and called to them two idle persons," and so returned, "two of them havyng forest bilies, the said Gay having the said long pyked staff, a hanger and a short dagger, and the residue of them having great axes in their hands."

By hewing "an olde lying tree within sound of the manor-house, they made Griffyth believe that they were felling trees, and when he came out, they attacked him and "a child" of sixteen who was with him. Gay may have been hurt in the fight, but Griffyth was knocked down and injured with a forest bill on the head and hand.

Finally he and the boy were taken three miles to the house of Lord Fitzwarren, who caused them to be "fetered" and put for two hours or more in his porter's lodge, whence they were released only on payment of a fee to the porter.

It is hard to say whether Gay's version or Griffyth's was the more truthful. Sir Andrew died in 1538 and was buried at East Quantoxhead, ancestral home of the Luttrells. An inscription there simply states:

"Here lies Andrew Luttrell, Knight, who departed the year of our lord God 1538 the 4th day of May on whose soul thou have mercy."

Easter Sepulchre monument post 1538 erected by order of the will of Sir Andrew Luttrell (1484–1538). It commemorates himself and his father Hugh Luttrell (died 1522). North wall of chancel, St Mary's Church, East Quantoxhead

'An olde lying tree within sound of the manor-house'. This tree was about 300 yards inside a wood to the left of the buildings.

CHAPTER 2

A HEROIC MOTHER
AND SON

During the English Civil War, Dunster Castle was besieged by the Parliamentarians under Col Blake, from Bridgwater. Two men from Dunster escaped to Oxford, where King Charles had his headquarters, and reported that the castle was relieved and the siege raised. The two men told Royalist soldiers that the besiegers, having used much violence to capture Col Wyndham's mother, had sent in their last summons to surrender and paraded the mother before the castle walls for all the garrison to witness thus:

"If you will yet deliver up the castle, you shall have fair quarter, if not, expect no mercy; your mother shall be at the very front to receive the first fury of your cannons: we expect your answer."

The Governor, Col Wyndham, replied, "If you do what

you threaten, you do the most barbarous act that was ever done; my mother I honour: but the cause I fight for the King, I honour more... Mother, do you forgive me and give me your blessing, and let the Rebells answer for spilling that blood of yours, which I would save with the loss of mine own, if I had enough blood for both master and yourself?" To this the mother answered "Son, I forgive thee, and pray God to blesse thee for this brave resolution; if I live I shall love thee the better for it; God's will be done."

Wyndham's mother fully expected to die there and then, but suddenly there appeared three notable cavaliers, Lord Wentworth, Sir Richard Grenville and Colonel Webb, who, summing up the perilous situation attacked the besiegers. They killed many, took a thousand prisoners, rescued the mother and relieved the castle.

This story has been repeated many times, mainly in ale houses. The Parliamentary Army, fearing their good name and discipline in Somerset soon denounced the tale as "a feeble lie" and "ale-house intelligence." In response their pamphlets became increasingly hostile towards Dunster Castle. "Dunster Castle stands accused of consorting with papists, breaking the Sabbath with ungodly pastimes and having now two priests of Baal within its walls" shouted one lurid headline.

CHAPTER 3

A 'MELANCHOLY ACCIDENT'

Caroline Luttrell was one of Col Francis Luttrell's nine children. Her eldest brother was George Luttrell, also of Kilve Court, who was to inherit Dunster Castle from her uncle, Henry Fownes Luttrell, in 1867. Her father, Col Francis, had in 1815 fought in single-handed combat with Jerome Bonaparte at the Battle of Waterloo, but he was away on military duty on the day of the accident. Caroline, who was 24 years old, had been entertaining at home in typical Victorian style.

The following report of Caroline's death appeared in the Taunton Courier on January 23rd 1856.

Melancholy Accident - on Thursday the 3rd inst, an accident which we regret to say has terminated fatally, happened to Miss Caroline Luttrell, daughter to Col Luttrell of Kilve, Somerset. It appears that on the above day a Christmas tree had been prepared and a candle placed on either side of the tree. Whilst the family and friends were sitting before the fire, Miss Luttrell, unknown to the others, withdrew and went into the drawing room for the purpose of lighting the candles by the side of the Christmas tree.

Whilst thus engaged, the flounce of her dress, which was of light material, caught fire, and she was soon enveloped in flames. Of course, assistance was speedily rendered, and Mr Edward Luttrell, her brother, in his efforts to save his sister, severely burnt his hand. Medical advice was soon obtained and everything done to alleviate the sufferings of the unfortunate young lady, but we regret to say that after having lingered in great suffering she expired on Tuesday last, much to the grief and regret of her family and friends.

This second report appeared in the *West Somerset Flying Post* on the 22nd January 1856.

Shocking death of Miss Caroline Luttrell – A Melancholy Accident

It is our painful duty to record the death of Miss Caroline Luttrell, second daughter of Col Luttrell of Kilve Court, in this county, from the shock and exhaustion caused by accidently setting fire to her dress, whilst lighting the tapers of a Christmas tree. It appears, that on Friday week, Mrs Luttrell – the gallant gentleman was away on duty with his regiment at Cork – entertained some friends at a family reunion and that one of the amusements of the evening was to be the distribution of presents from a Christmas tree.

During the evening the deceased young lady left the circle for the purpose of lighting the tapers on the tree and desired none of the party to visit the room until she had rung the bell. To ensure that no intruders would enter, Miss Luttrell turned the key of the door and commenced lighting up the tree. Unfortunately she commenced lighting the lower tapers first and then reaching up to light those on the higher branches her thin evening dress caught fire and she was immediately enveloped in flames.

It appears the deceased ran to the bell and pulled it violently and afterwards unlocked the door and proceeded towards the room where the company was assembled; on meeting her surrounded by flames and smoke, their horror it may be conceived was extreme; her brother, assisted by others, with great difficulty extinguished the flames, but not until after receiving a severe burn on the hand.

Medical assistance was immediately sent for. Miss Luttrell's eye-lids, face and neck were found to have suffered most from the flames, but it was at first hoped that no fatal result would follow. The exhaustion, however, and shock caused to the system was too great, and on the Monday she died. The deceased was in her 25th year, an amiable lady and greatly beloved. This melancholy event has thrown the most painful gloom over a wide circle, and the family's distress is sympathised in by the whole of the neighbourhood.

CHAPTER 4

THE LEGEND OF GRISEL GRIS AND THE KNIGHT

At the onset of the Hundred Years War with France, John de Mohun V fought alongside Edward, The Black Prince, in a division that had "all the flower of English chivalry within it" and after the Battle of Crécy in 1346, for bravery shown on the field of battle, Edward presented to Sir John a beautiful warhorse whom he called Grisel Gris (grey tint).

During the medieval period there was only one approach to the castle: up through Sir Hugh Luttrell's gatehouse, where, after passing under its vaulted archway, carriages, horsemen and those on foot had to turn abruptly to the right through Sir Reynold de Mohun's impressive gateway, then veer to the left, still ascending, to reach the front of castle.

From first to last the road was exceedingly steep, so

great skill was required to drive a carriage safely through when descending to the town. Accidents must have been numerous, not least fatal ones.

On returning to Dunster Castle after one battle Sir John brought with him his prized possession, his warhorse. One cold winter's morning he was exercising two of his other horses in the old medieval deer park, or hanger park, when he gave a shrill whistle which Grisel Gris knew to be from his master.

The horse, which had been grazing on the 'castle dispasture' area (now Green Court), reared and immediately turned and raced down the slope, through the 13th century Gateway, over the wooden bridge spanning the dry ditch, then veered left to descend the hill and stumbled on the icy path as it tried to negotiate the sharp bend. Tradition says that it 'dashed its brains out' when it crashed headlong into the retaining stone wall just past the outer arch of the gatehouse.

It was Sir John's wife, Lady Joan de Mohun, who eventually sold the castle to the Luttrell family, and the slippery slope down to the stables continue to be the cause of mishaps to this day.

CHAPTER 5

A HOARD OF GOLD

Thomas Luttrell had had a chequered career which was
every bit as exciting as that of his elder brother, Sir John
Luttrell, and fought alongside him during the wars in
Scotland 1547-1550 and alongside their uncle, Thomas
Wyndham, in the same wars. He also assisted with
collecting Sir John's army and money for the war.

His marriage to Margaret Hadley of Withycombe
during the ecclesiastical lax reign of Edward VI was
challenged when 'Bloody' Mary succeeded in 1553. They
were accused of being first cousins and the marriage was
deemed null and void. Thomas had to petition Rome, and
a solemn document issued by the Cardinal of St Angelo,
Papal Penitentiary, at St Peter's on the 28th November
1558 recites that Thomas Luttrell esquire and Margaret
Hadley had, by their petition, confessed that they had,
without proper dispensation, been actually married,
although related in the third of third, and in the third and

fourth degrees of kindred, and although spiritually related, the mother of Thomas (Dame Margaret Wyndham, portrait in Inner Hall) having stood godmother to Margaret at her baptism or confirmation.

The language of the document leaves it doubtful whether the marriage had been solemnized in public and whether any issue had been actually born. Its effect, however, was to release the parties from the excommunication that they had incurred on condition of a fresh marriage "in the face of the (Catholic) Church, and to legitimate any previous offspring".

The dispensation, having been issued a few days after the accession of Queen Elizabeth I, was probably one of the very last documents of its kind despatched before the final break between England and Rome, and the sequel is perhaps the most curious part of the story.

For nearly two years no further action was taken in the matter, but on the 27th August 1560, Thomas Luttrell was solemnly married in the church at East Quantoxhead, his bride being described in the register as "Mrs Margaret Hadley". Their eldest son, George Luttrell (The Builder) was born the following month, but in the inscription which he set up in memory of his parents some sixty years later, it expressly stated that Thomas Luttrell and Margaret Hadley "were lawfully married".

Thomas Luttrell lived most of the time at Marshwood, near Blue Anchor, which can still be seen today. He is described in further legal proceedings as "Thomas Luttrell of Marshwood" when a dispute regarding treasure trove arose in the Hundred of Carhampton.

These are the brief main facts of the case. A certain Agnes Ellesworth, the wife of Richard Ellesworth the Elder, "of Imberscombe [Timberscombe], husbandman," was delivered of a stillborn child in the month of May 1559, at Owl Knowle in the parish of Carhampton, a house which it is thought he rented from Luttrell's cousin Thomas Trevelyan of Nettlecombe Court.

The following is reported:

Agnes, in digging a grave hard by in which to bury the infant body, suddenly came upon a great quantity of gold coins, sufficient, it was estimated, to fill a "wyne quart", less a quarter of a "wyne pint". After giving a few coins to two female friends who were with her at the time, she put the rest into a "trene dysshe" (wooden dish) and so handed them over to her husband Richard on his return. They consisted of "old nobles" and "half old nobles" and he reckoned the noble at 13s 4d. estimated their value at £107. 10s.

When a report of the discovery reached Thomas Luttrell, he immediately laid claim to the gold as treasure trove in his Hundred of Carhampton, but was satisfied to claim the coins to the value of £100. Agnes was not to gain the remainder, £7 10s. and they were handed over, in May 1560, to Sir Thomas Parry, Treasurer of the Queen's Household.

Then began claim and counter claim in the Exchequer, as the Attorney General put forward the right of the Crown and Thomas Luttrell defended his own claim to be supported by extracts from court rolls and bailiffs' accounts. Eventually the

*case was set down for trial before the justices of assize at Chard
in July 1564.*

Here the story ends abruptly. There is no record of the

A pot of gold

St John the Baptist Church, Carhampton. Owl Knowle, where Agnes dug the
grave for her child and found the coins, is close by.

judgement which was to have been entered at the Exchequer at Michaelmas term. Perhaps the Crown withdrew its claim. Anyhow the Luttrells have maintained theirs ever since, and it is interesting to note that there were at Dunster Castle a number of nobles, half nobles and angels from the reign of Edward VI which were presumably the remains of the hoard of gold found at Owl Knowle in 1559. But this was the late 1800s. The coins are no longer at the castle.

CHAPTER 6

A PAIR OF WIVES FROM HELL

The unfortunate marital choices of George Luttrell

George Luttrell, who altered the medieval castle to become a Jacobean mansion in the early 17th century, married twice, and neither of his brides were popular with the rest of the Luttrell family, to put it mildly. But first a word on George himself.

One deposition described him as 'a very great and potent gentleman [who] published [that he was prepared] to spend £5,000 ... to terrify and dismay his opponent'. He brought an action against a widowed copyholder to find out if she lost her estate through incontinence, and claimed the property of his second cousin on the ground that he was a bastard. He sent his bailiff to take livestock from reluctant tenants, and, in one dispute, used force to help secure the £5 relief on a knight's fee which had become due 25 years before. Surprisingly, a contemporary document refers to him as 'much noted for his hospitality and the general love and respect of his neighbours'. But even his architect, William Arnold, had to sue him to obtain his money.

In October the young couple were solemnly contacted at Marsh "by words of the present time", he taking her by the hand and saying, "I, George, take thee, Joan, to my wedded wife, and thereto I give thee my faith and troth", though she eventually became the mother of his twelve children.

Joan Stewkeley, his first wife, was also his cousin. She was the daughter of his guardian, Hugh Stewkeley, who had to endure harsh words from George's grandmother, Dame Margaret Wyndham (see part 1, chapter 4). Apparently George was determined to marry her to put an end to the 'brabblings' and noisy quarrelsome arguments between her father and Dame Margaret, who declared her grandson would be "utterly cast away" if he were to marry the daughter of a miserly lawyer who had so often in the past made trouble for the Luttrells. She also stated that she would take away the Priory of Dunster from him and make him "a poor gentleman". Sir James Fitzjames from Wales, who wanted George to marry his own niece instead, waded in and agreed with Dame Margaret by publicly stating that Joan Stewkely was "a slutte and that she had no good qualities". Though she was mother of his twelve children.

After Joan's death in 1621, a mere ten months later George Luttrell was married at Court House, East Quantoxhead, the Luttrell ancestral home, to "an obscure person" by the name of Silvestra Capps, daughter of James Capps of Jews in Wiveliscombe. Silvestra Capps (Luttrell) had for her jointure the manors of Kilton and East Quantoxhead. A leaden pipe-head at the latter place bears her initials with those of her husband, and the date 1628. The arms of Luttrell impaling those of Capps are also to be seen at the Luttrell Arms Hotel at Dunster. The whole house had apparently been altered for her benefit.

It was Silvestra who persuaded George Luttrell to expand the existing building with the addition of the south-west wing and new porch. The expansion and improvements which left the house largely in the form it exists today were completed by 1628. After Capps' death in 1655 the house was leased as a farmhouse, and although some minor damage was done during the next few hundred years when it was used as a granary, the only structural alteration was the addition of a door at wagon level to enable loading and unloading.[4] In the 1860s

The arms of Luttrell impaling those of Capps are also to be seen above entrance porch at the Luttrell Arms Hotel in Dunster village.

Photograph by Rachel Shaw 2007. New porch and south-west wing
added by Silvestra Capps

quarter sessions were held at the house, and it has been known as Court House ever since.

Little is known of Silvestra's life with George, but given her reputation for being "greedy, unpleasant and common" it was anything but harmonious. This can be borne out by what happened when George Luttrell died. As her jointure she obtained the manors of Kilton and East Quantoxhead and lived at Court House with successive husbands until her death in 1655. Her character is shown most clearly, and sinister, in the words of her second husband's will, Sir Edmond Skory:

To Dame Sylvestra Skory, my wife, whom I heartily forgive all her wicked attempts against me, a praier book called 'The Practice of Piety', desiring that she better love and affect the same than hitherto she has done and to my servant George Baker, who hath lived under the tyranny of my wife, 20s.

Silvestra tried, in vain, to prove that her dead husband had been of unsound mind. Yet a persistent story survives of the time the hapless Sir Edmund Skory fell foul of her rage and Silvestra rushed at him and threw him out of a top window at Court House. A lady with a temper indeed!

George Luttrell remained active until Charles I's reign, being buried at Dunster on April 23 1629. His will left the bulk of his property first to his wife, who remarried twice and was still living in 1655, and then to his heir, Thomas. A codicil added shortly before his death provided £140 for the poor of Dunster.

Effigy of Joan Stewkley, St George's Church, Dunster

CHAPTER 7

THE LEGEND OF THE BAREFOOT LADY

A night on the moors

One of the best-known ladies of Dunster Castle is Lady Joan de Mohun, wife of that most illustrious knight Sir John de Mohun V, and the subject of part 1 chapter 2. It is worth noting that on the only occasion since the Norman Conquest on which Dunster Castle has changed ownership through sale, it was sold by one widow and bought by another. It would be interesting to know how the purchaser, Lady Luttrell, contrived to raise so large a sum, and how she paid it over, although it probably was not all in the coin of the realm. The actual legend goes like this:

There was once a tyrant lord of Dunster Castle who was cruel, vengeful and mean. He would tax the people of the village until they had no money left. Some of the villagers approached the lord's wife, Lady Joan, who was as kind and compassionate as he was evil. They asked her to petition her husband not to raise taxes any higher.

Lady Joan, in her gentle way, begged the lord to consider the poor plight of the inhabitants and not to raise taxes any

more. The lord, in a wild temper, shouted to Joan that if she wanted to help the poor so much then he would give to them as much common land for their own use as she could walk barefoot in one night.

Joan set forth barefoot on a cold winter's evening to try to obtain as much land as she could for the villagers. She had been stumbling for several hours when

Illustration of Joan, barefoot in medieval peasant dress

Landscape at Dunster Castle, the scene Lady Joan is said to have traversed one cold winter's evening Picture by Julia Amies Green

suddenly she fell fainting next to a stream. Some menfolk, who were keeping an eye on the lady because of the darkness, rushed to her aid and begged her not to continue this perilous journey, but Joan simply looked up at them and whispered, "I must go on". The villagers were shocked to find her in such a condition, but her determination shone through and she bravely walked on until she completed a full circle around the old deer park and the slopes of Grabbist and Conigar, returning exhausted to the castle and into the arms of her waiting husband. The lord kept his word, no taxes were raised and the poor got to keep all the common land Lady Joan had traversed that very evening.

From Devon Notes and Queries, vol iv. P. 252, Legend of a Barefoot Pilgrim:

Three history chroniclers, Camden, Gerard and Fuller all agree in stating that Lady Joan de Mohun of Dunster Castle had obtained from her husband Sir John as much common ground for the inhabitants of the village as she could walk round barefoot in one day. The story, which reminds us of partly of Dido and partly of Godiva, might be dismissed as fanciful were it not for the fact that these writers had access to a chronicle of the Mohun family composed in the lifetime of this lady and actually dedicated to her.

CHAPTER 8

LUCY LUTTRELL AND THE MISSING GOLD

Lucy Luttrell (?-1718) was the granddaughter of John Pym of Brymore, near Bridgwater, a great Parliamentarian leader. She married Francis Luttrell on October 1655, at Buckland Monachorum, Devonshire. Lucy's aunt was Lady Drake of Buckland Abbey,* with whom she was staying at the time of wedding. Jane Popham, wife of Thomas Luttrell of Dunster Castle, was Lucy's mother-in-law. Jane, apparently, had already made a will in favour of Lucy's son, Alexander Luttrell, having promised to make the boy a good man, but things did not go according to plan.

On the death of Jane Luttrell of Marshwood, Blue Anchor, in 1688, Lucy Luttrell became involved in lawsuits at the Somerset Assizes, in the Court of Exchequer and in the Chancery itself, the highest court of judicature next to the House of Lords. She was acting on behalf of her young son, Alexander, commonly called 'Sany'. Jane, his old grandmother who had resolutely defended Dunster Castle during the recent Civil War, had undertaken to provide for the boy and had duly made a will in his favour: "She hoped to make Sany (Alexander) almost as good a man as his elder brother: saying that if his elder brother invited him to dinner, he should be able to invite his elder brother to supper."

But Jane seems to have had a somewhat miserly disposition, for instead of buying land or otherwise investing her money (for Sany), she amassed "a great treasure of gold and silver at Marshwood for, in 1667, the good people of Stoke Courci apprehended nine persons well horsed and armed who had confessed before the magistrates a design of robbing her house".

Marshwood Farm, near Blue Anchor

At her death however, only £150 was found there out of £10,000 she was believed to have hoarded. At the instigation of Lucy Luttrell, two of the servants were indicted of felony, and at a later stage, Lucy charged her own sister-in-law Amy and her husband, George Reynall, with having "caused large sums of money in bags to be secretly moved from Marshwood".

The Reynells were eventually condemned in £6000 with £200 costs and George Reynell was imprisoned in the Fleet and later, Marshalsea Prison. After his escape from the latter, Lucy sued the Marshall and Keeper of the Gaol and obtained judgement to the sum of £6,200. Lucy Luttrell survived until Christmas Eve 1718 and was buried at Dunster on 7th January 1719.

Buckland Monachorum Abbey, 1823, National Trust. Buckland Abbey, now with the National Trust, was once the home where Sir Francis Drake stayed after the Battle of Cadiz and the Armada in 1588.

CHAPTER 9

THE MARRIAGE THAT CHANGED THE LAW

Anne Luttrell was the daughter of Simon Luttrell of Luttrellstown, near Dublin, Ireland, who claimed descent from the original stock of Luttrells, including the Somerset branch. Simon was raised to the peerage of Ireland in 1768 and was created Baron Irnham in 1781. When further honours were conferred on him he became Viscount Carhampton and, in 1785, the Earl of Carhampton. Elizabeth Luttrell, eldest daughter of Simon and sister of the Duchess of Cumberland, Lady Anne Frederick, was sarcastically called 'Princess Elizabeth', being a coarse, unprincipled woman who was devoured by a love of play.

The Royal Marriage Act of 1772 required the Sovereign's approval for marriages involving the Royal Family. This Act was rushed through Parliament in response to the elopement and marriage of King George III's brother, Henry Frederick, Duke of Cumberland, at Calais in 1771, to Anne Luttrell, without informing the King. George III was outraged at this union and would have stopped it if he had been able to. In order to prevent any further regal embarrassment, the Act was introduced when the king heard that Anne had been described as a woman "very loose with her favours" and Horace Walpole, Prime Minister, commented: "She had for many months

been dallying with the Duke's passions, till she had fixed him to more serious views than he had intended".

The Duke's marriage to the commoner Lady Anne Luttrell (1743-1808)

Anne Luttrell was painted by Thomas Gainsborough several times, the first in 1766 as 'Mrs Anne Horton', the wife of a relatively obscure member of the gentry. The next time she was painted by him, in 1777, she was the wife of a royal prince, a quite dramatic transformation. This painting of Anne Luttrell now forms part of the Queen's Collection.

on October 2, 1771 was the catalyst for the Royal Marriages Act 1772, which forbids any descendant of George II to marry without the monarch's permission. There were no children from this marriage. Lady Anne, though from a good family — she was a daughter of Simon Luttrell, Earl of Carhampton, and the widow of Christopher Horton of Catton Hall - will be forever famous, not only for her beauty, which was unsurpassed in a day when beauty was at its highest standard, but for her marriage to the Duke of Cumberland, which brought about all the stir and commotion of the Royal Marriage Act.

Anne had been married when a mere girl in her teens to Christopher Horton, a sporting squire, of whom little is known save that he was owner of Catton Park, Derbyshire. After a few years he died, leaving his widow a moderate provision, though it was not a quarter sufficient to satisfy her extravagant tastes. She was 24, with bewitching eyes, which, when she pleased, she could animate to enchantment. "Her coquetry was so active, so varied, and yet so habitual, that it was difficult not to see through it, and yet as difficult to resist it," said Horace Walpole, English historian, a Member of Parliament, connoisseur, playwright and novelist. He described her as a coquette beyond measure, "artful as Cleopatra and complete mistress of her passions and projects". "Indeed," he added, "eyelashes three-quarters of a yard shorter would have served to conquer such a head as she has turned." He went on:

For all that, Horace was mightily well pleased when his

niece, the beautiful Lady Waldegrave, made the conquest of the Duke of Gloucester, whose mental abilities were much on a par with those of his brother, the Duke of Cumberland.

Anne Luttrell met the Duke, it is said, at a boarding-house, where he had gone until the scandal of one of his numerous love affairs had blown over. He was no match for the beautiful widow, whose dancing of the minuet completely carried his slight defences, and, finding she was impervious to any proposal save orthodox marriage, he followed her to Calais, where the knot was tied hard and fast, all legal forms being duly executed, and no loophole left through which the royal captive could wriggle.

The Duchess did not gain all she expected. The Royal Marriage Act indeed could not separate her from the Duke, or take from her the title of Duchess, but these advantages (especially the first) hardly repaid her for the snubs of the Court and for the isolation of her life, this latter lasting many years, the nobility being too good courtiers to risk irritating their Majesties by paying any deference to the interloper into the royal circle.

Later, the Duchess and her husband took a fiendish method of retaliation. When the Prince of Wales (afterwards George IV) came to man's estate, the Duchess wove her toils about him so as to attain great influence over his easily-governed mind; neither she nor the Duke made any secret that their object was to intimidate the party into receiving the Duchess, and the plan succeeded. Although not publicly recognized, she had the entrée to the more intimate family circle.

Her triumph, however, did not last long, as much of her

glory was shorn when the Duke died in 1790. From that time we get only occasional glimpses of the beautiful Duchess, who survived her husband some twenty years.

Anne died on 28th Dec 1808 at Trieste, Italy, and is buried there.

Another contemporary account states that her sister Elizabeth Luttrell:

...had been imprisoned in the Fleet for gambling debts; gave a hairdresser £50 to marry her, but which, according to the then state of the debtors law, enabled her to procure a release. Fled abroad to Germany where she was convicted of picking pockets, was again sentenced, and condemned to clean the streets chained to a wheelbarrow so as not to run away.

On the 11th of March 1797, her Ladyship (Lady Buckinghamshire), together with Lady E. Luttrell and a Mrs Stuart, were convicted at the Marlborough Street Police-court, in the penalty of £50, for playing at the game of Faro; and Henry Martindale was convicted in the sum of £200, for keeping the Faro table at Lady Buckinghamshire's. The witnesses had been servants of her Ladyship, recently discharged on account of a late extraordinary loss of 500 guineas from her Ladyship's house, belonging to the Faro bank.

One wag commented that Elizabeth Luttrell was "The Duke of Grafton's mistress, the Duke of Dorset's mistress and every Duke's mistress".

The unfortunate woman is widely believed to have

poisoned herself in later life. Not the sort of sister-in-law the king would have wanted.

The stage play *Bad Lady Betty* by W. D. Scull (Matthews) in three acts, is a clever and powerful play and gives an animated picture of Lady Elizabeth Luttrell, the sister of the Duchess of Cumberland, and of other Luttrells of Four Oaks. The historical print edition of the drama is at The British Library.

April 2006 saw the nuptials of Prince Charles and Mrs Camilla Parker Bowles. When the happy event was announced mention was made of the Royal Marriage Act, which required that Charles seek permission from the Queen beforehand.

Walk in Kew Garden, by Thomas Gainsborough. Duke and Duchess of Cumberland and Anne Luttrell with her sister Lady Elizabeth. The picture hangs in the corridor at Windsor Castle (Royal Collection).

CHAPTER 10

TALES FROM SIR WALTER'S MEMOIRS

The following accounts have been taken from Sir Walter Luttrell's memoirs, Court House 1995, and compiled by John Fleming, National Trust Sound Archives, 1996.

Riding sidesaddle

When Walter was asked if his mother rode, she replied that she was a beautiful rider, almost entirely sidesaddle. She used to ride astride in Australia, but she always hunted sidesaddle and went like an absolute rocket! She had a lot of crashing falls in Australia riding the virtually unbroken horses out there and she had a very bad back, which used to play her up. No one ever had a horse box in those days and we used to meet up at Ralegh's Cross and ride for two hours. She often asked me to ride her horse on, when I used to take the pommel out and sling a leg loose and just walk or jog.

There was one occasion when I was out on foot with the Minehead Harriers and she was riding when her back suddenly gave way. I was at a gate, having opened it for her, and she asked me if I would take the horse on. The horse was called Peacock, and I had ridden him lots of times. I climbed up, but of course it was sidesaddle. I had ridden a lot but I must say I had never been so frightened in my life. If you look down on the right hand side it is like looking down from Beachy Head, with nothing between you and Mother Earth! However we had a very good hunt, and at least I can claim I have once ridden to hounds side saddle!

My mother was a very good whip. She used to drive during the war and then went on after the war, and that was great fun because she had a superbly smart high dog cart with a lovely skewbald pony, which was also extremely smart. By then there was nothing else in the stables and she kept on our stud groom, who was Reg Godby, a great character who had really nothing else to do except look after this pony, which was called Jigsaw, polish the trap and harness and his own boots and gaiters. Consequently the whole thing was absolutely immaculate.

She used to drive into Minehead up until three or four years before she died. This was much to our terror because the traffic then was terrific, although it did not seem to bother her. It was a great sight. My father was dead by that time and I started opening the castle first for one day and then two days a week. We used to get very big crowds round, and one thing that everybody really loved was to see the dog cart arrive at a spanking pace. It used to come up around the front to the front door and my mother used to emerge, absolutely happy with a great garden hat on with a basket for whatever she was going to buy in Minehead. Reg used to stand at the pony's head, because he was very fresh. Reg would take a flying leap on board and off they would go, trotting down the drive and the visitors thought it was the best thing ever, much better than going round the castle! Reg had a wonderful long white coat with gold buttons – it was a magnificent sight.

Morning Room madness

My mother's desk was always here (the Morning Room) and she used to work quite a lot at night, and it was only about 1936, 1937 and she had her dogs up here, and then one day, it was very late, sort of midnight, and suddenly the dogs... all their hackles came up and they came up to this door here (door to stairhall), and they didn't actually bark but they just stood there and she told them not to be so stupid, but they wouldn't come away.

So she came round and opened this door, which was shut, and there was our Head Housemaid then, standing at this bottom step, brandishing an enormous great carving knife and making all the swipes in the air, and she said, "They're here, they're all around me, can't you see them madam?" So she (mother) said, "No I can't", then the maid made another great swipe, you know, and my mother stood back a bit, and realised that she'd gone round the bend. However, she said, "No, no, they're not here at all." You know. "Oh, yes they are."

Anyway mother somehow got her up to her bedroom, which is way up above here, a maid's room, and managed to put her in and shut the door, then she (maid) went away, I'm afraid with a man in a white coat in a van. Mad as a coot! But she'd suddenly gone round the bend. But this is where it all happened. I think my mother was very brave. I'd have run screaming. You don't argue with a cook's knife.

Hermione in Love
Hermione Luttrell, née Gunston, wrote:

I was born in London and lived in London all my life until I married. My father, who died when I was eleven, was on the Stock Exchange, and we lived north of the park in Southwark Crescent. After his death we went to live in Canning Place, which is a small street with houses originally built for the ladies-in-waiting of Queen Anne.

During the war, the presence of a landmine in the vicinity made the house virtually uninhabitable and my mother took a cottage in the country. I, by then, was doing a secretarial course and subsequently working. I lived with friends for a while until my mother returned to town and took a flat in Mount Street.

It was then I met Walter. His parents were old friends of my family. We got engaged within three days of meeting each other and we were married two days later! Not a thing I would recommend to anyone else, but in our case it worked out perfectly.

I was nineteen and about to go into the Wrens, having been accepted. But it seemed that a service career would not be compatible with young married life, especially with a husband constantly on the move. In fact he was in Northumberland then and we managed during that first year to live out in various cottages.

When it was no longer possible for wives to be in proximity with their husbands' regiments I got a job with S.O.E. in Baker Street. Special Operations Executive was a British Secret Service, formed in 1940 to encourage resistance to Hitler's Germany.

Sir Walter remembers:

My unit trained for various armoured roles including amphibious tanks and were on standby for going to the Middle East, but we were never sent there. During a spell of training in Northumberland in 1942, I came down to London for a long weekend's leave and met Hermione Gunston for the first time on the Friday evening. We got engaged before I returned to my Regiment on the following Tuesday.

We were married in London three days before Christmas and after spending Christmas in

Gloucestershire we came back to Dunster for a week of parties, introductions, etc. By no means a peaceful honeymoon!

From a flat in Sloane Street, Hermione Luttrell worked for the SOE (Special Operations Executive) until the end of the war through the V1 and V2 bombings and inevitable shortages. On August the 6th 1945 at 8:15 am, the uranium atom bomb exploded 580 metres above the city of Hiroshima with a blinding flash, creating a fireball and sending surface temperatures to 4,000 °C. Fierce heat and radiation burst out in every direction, unleashing a high pressure shockwave. It vaporised tens of thousands of people and animals, melted buildings and street cars and reduced a 400-year-old city to dust. World War 2 had come to an end, and with it Hermione's job.

Hermione Hamilton Gunston was the daughter of Cecil Bernard Gunston and Lady Doris Gwendoline Blackwood. She married Colonel Sir Geoffrey Walter Fownes Luttrell, son of Geoffrey Luttrell, on 23 December 1942. Between May 1991 and October 1994, she was company director of East Quantoxhead Trust Company and company director of Somerset Gardens Trust. She lived in 2003 at Court House, East Quantoxhead. She died on 9 March 2009, almost two years after the death of Sir Walter.

Treasure hunts and steam engines

Mother [Alys Luttrell] organised all the children's parties in the summertime, and would lay on treasure hunts, which at Dunster, around the grounds, were simply wonderful. Then she would arrange for different sorts of races, you know, egg and spoon races and all that sort of thing out on the lawn, where parties of twelve, fourteen or twenty school chums would arrive. But really all we wanted to do was go down the estate yard to see - and if possible, get on board - one of the steam engines or the steam roller.

The drivers were frightfully good and very kind and they always let us all in and sometimes even let us drive it a few yards. It's not the cleanest of jobs. And all the girls in their party frocks and party dresses, used to go back covered in oil, and they weren't terribly popular. But still, it was a lovely thing, and, I think, my only claim to fame. I mean other families had wonderful treasure hunts and probably bigger teas and bigger everythings, but nobody else had a steam roller they could play with.

Mother used to let us all go down to the Yard to just play around and we loved that because there were the Shire horses and we had this very big stable, or my grandfather did, of Shire horses for the timber. My father's own farm ones

Alys greeting guests at a private function in the castle

were down at a different place, down at the bottom of Dunster. But I think there were, if I remember rightly, about fourteen in at one time. And if you went down in the evenings, they used to finish work at five, and they were getting their evening feed, and it was a pretty magnificent sight even without all their harness and everything on, they were lovely.

And of course, when it came round to show time, like Dunster Show, there was always tremendous rivalry between my father's team of farm horses and my grandfather's team of timber horses. And the two rival head drover's team were always ready to beat either the young Squire or the old Squire. I think the judges used to cheat: they used to give prizes alternate years I think, but still, it was great fun.

Alice, Sir Walter's grandmother and Alys Luttrell, his mother, on entrance porch stairs at Dunster Castle

The butler, Lady Alice and the thrush

The butler was inherited by my parents, chap called Padfield, a superb butler. One day mother said to him: "Oh, Padfield, I think we could have a marmalade pot, it is very near the bottom." Padfield looked at her rather surprised: "As you like Madam, but the late Mrs Luttrell ALWAYS liked everything finished before we refilled".

There is another story of my grandmother having been a bit of a terror. Every morning in winter, after breakfast, she used to feed the birds out of the Dining Room window. One morning she made her usual mixture of what was left of the porridge and bits of toast and anything else, I expect, odd bits of bacon or whatever was left over, made

Alice Edwina Luttrell

THE LADIES OF DUNSTER CASTLE

all this mush up into a bowl, threw up the sash window, and threw it out and called out as usual, "Birdie, birdie, birdie," and out it went.

And the poor wretched, brand-new garden boy – a chap called Charlie Thrush, who'd just arrived and it was his first morning on – caught the whole lot, slap on the top of his head. He let out some awful oaths, cursing and swearing, so she looked out and said,

"Good gracious! What's your name, boy?"

"Thrush, madam."

"Don't be so impertinent!" she said, and banged the window shut. She was a formidable old lady.

Mary Luttrell in the First World War

The Great War involved even the smallest and remotest of Exmoor communities, where every memorial serves as a reminder of the 11,281 Somerset men, eleven from Dunster alone, who lost their lives. At the start of the Great War many of the volunteers in West Somerset were young farm workers from villages like Dunster. Agriculture had been in recession and the army offered three good meals a day, a warm uniform and a real prospect of a quick war.

In September 1914, soon after the outbreak of the war, a recruitment drive was held at the Dunster Parish meeting with Alexander Luttrell, a veteran of the Rifle Brigade, addressing those gathered. The West Somerset Free Press reported:

A recruiting meeting was held on Wednesday night in the Parish Room, Alexander Fownes Luttrell presiding and giving an address. Other addresses being given by the Rev Preb Hancock and Sergt. Hunt, B Company 5th Battalion, Somerset Light Infantry. The following eight names were given in (joined up): Ambrose Thomas, Arthur Taylor, Frank Winter, Samuel Thomas, Herbert Sydenham, John Griffiths, Charles Griffiths, John Kerslake, William Thrush, R. G. Hayden, J.M. Williams.

In a rousing speech Alexander evoked the memory of his grandfather, Lt Col Francis Luttrell, and his heroics in 1815 at the Battle of Waterloo. He was reported to have been engaged in hand-to-hand fighting with Jerome Bonaparte, Napoleon's brother, and was wounded there in the orchard at Huguenot Farm. Alexander, to standing applause from the audience, further stated that it was essential that Germany should be defeated on land first and foremost hence this appeal for troops. Lord St Audries said that the meeting and subsequent recruitment went 'splendidly'.

Of the enlisted men at that meeting in 1914 one name stands out in particular; William Thrush. This is the same teenage boy who had a brief run in with Alys Luttrell when she threw her breakfast crumbs and mash out of the Dining Room window for the birds and hit a boy named Thrush instead.

Whilst the war raged on in France the village pulled together to get through these times of rationing. The Public Elementary School, which was commissioned by

George Luttrell, now Dunster First School, helped with food production:

There was little outward change in the running of the school at first. A flagstaff was erected in the playground and gardening classes were started in the spring of 1915. The school garden became an important addition to village horticulture production and seeds were provided annually by the County Council. Only the boys were involved in the garden work and when horses broke into the garden from the adjoining fields, destroying the valuable crops, permission was immediately sought by the school governors to obtain barbed wire fencing to protect the garden from further depredations. In November 1915 a collection was held in the school to provide Christmas presents for the soldiers and sailors. By order of the County Education Committee the afternoon classes were altered to 1:30pm – 3:30pm for the duration of the War and the timetable adjusted to suit. In November 1916 the pupils held another collection, this time to provide Christmas Puddings for Somerset Soldiers. One year later the children were allowed time away from lessons to help with the harvest: and for the School, a Certificate of Merit for Gardening was received and framed. November 11th 1918 and the Armistice is signed. After being told the wonderful news the children were dismissed and granted a holiday.

Just prior to WWI the militant ladies' movement the Suffragettes flooded into Minehead and Dunster during the local elections. Their founder, Emmeline Pankhurst, herself visited the two small towns. She addressed a massed rally in Minehead and spoke for over one hour in

Minehead and Dunster Voluntary Aid Detachment staff, 1915

stifling conditions. Later they held an open-air meeting in Wellington Square, where they had advertised by chalking notices on all the town's pavements and in the evening staged a gathering at the Yarn Market in Dunster. It is very probable that Mary Luttrell of Dunster Castle would have met her.

Alexander Luttrell returned to his civic duties as a JP, presiding over the Dunster Petty Sessions on the first Friday of each month. During this time he gave a local man three months' hard labour after he was found guilty of stealing ladies' underwear from washing lines at Minehead Quay. Police say that when they confronted him he admitted to the crime and had several pairs of knickers on his person! Apparently this was not the first time he had been caught doing this. On another occasion he cautioned seven youths from Minehead who were causing a disturbance in Blenheim Road by singing ragtime songs.

Mary Luttrell, George Luttrell's eldest daughter, wasted no time in helping with the war effort and joined the Red Cross Society in August 1914. She sent a letter to the West Somerset Free Press the day after war was declared which stated, *"Somerset has nobly appointed the Red Cross Society in its devoted & self-sacrificing work for our wounded soldiers".*

She also called a meeting at Minehead where she urged all to follow the advice of Queen Mary about the vital importance of the society at this time. Mary was ordered to coordinate Voluntary Aid Detachments (VAD) and also to fit up her large dwelling (Dunster Castle) and be ready to receive orders for mobilisation and hold themselves in readiness to receive patients; there were 3000 such auxiliary hospitals in England. Minehead Town Hall was

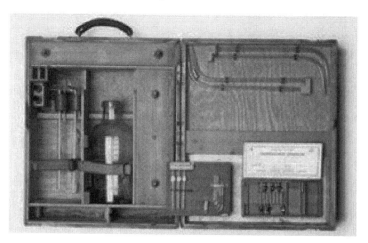

Blood transfusion kit 1914-1918

turned into a VAD hospital and an armoury was established at the Drill Hall in Quay Lane. Mary stayed in West Somerset during the war to help those in need, working closely with the Red Cross Society. In 1921 Alexander Luttrell erected the Dunster Memorial Hall in memory of those Dunster men who had fought and died in World War I.

Between the two World Wars the VAD was reorganised and its role changed to one of supporting the medical services, which included the ability to volunteer to mobilise with the Territorial Army. They could also work in roles such as nurses, radiographers, pharmacists, clerks and laboratory assistants.

During WWII many women became VADs when they were already overseas, such as in the Far East where they may have been accompanying their husbands during peacetime. Some became prisoners of the Japanese. Numbers for those employed in Britain, which included those to be posted abroad, were broken down as 14,155 from the Red Cross, 1695 from the Order of St John's Cross and 21 from the St Andrew's Ambulance Association.

Printed in Great Britain
by Amazon